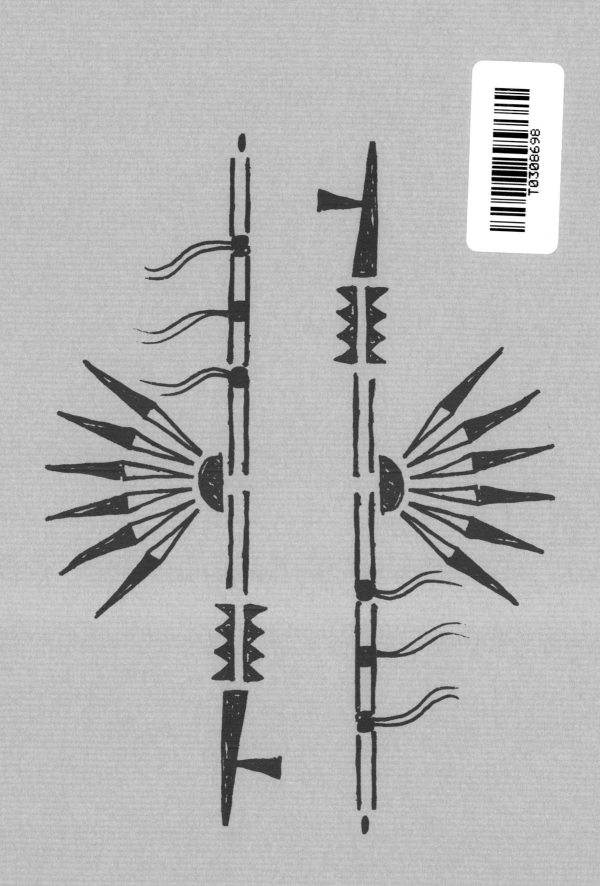

THE FEATHERED SUN

FRITHJOF SCHUON

THE
FEATHERED
SUN

PLAINS INDIANS IN ART AND PHILOSOPHY

WORLD WISDOM BOOKS

Articles appearing in this book were translated from French. English translations
have previously appeared in the following publications: "The Symbolist Outlook,"
Tomorrow (London), Vol. 14, No. 2, Spring 1966; "The Shamanism of the Red Indians,"
Light on the Ancient Worlds, World Wisdom Books (Bloomington) 1984; "The Sacred Pipe of the
Red Indians," *Language of the Self,* Ganesh & Co. (Madras) 1959; "The Demiurge in
North American Mythology," *Logic and Transcendence,* Harper & Row (New York) 1975;
"The Sun Dance," *Esoterism as Principle and as Way,* Perennial Books (London) 1981;
"His Holiness and the Red Indian," *Sankara and Shanmata,* (Madras) 1969. Material in
"Excerpts from a Diary" was translated from German. Material in "Excerpts from
Correspondence" was translated from German and French.

Library of Congress Cataloging-in-Publication Data

Schuon, Frithjof, 1907-
The feathered sun: plains Indians in art and philosophy

ISBN 0-941532-08-9 Hardcover 37.50   ISBN 0-941532-10-0 Papercover 25.00
1. Plains Indians—Art. 2. Plains Indians—Philosophy.
3. Plains Indians—Religion and mythology.   I. Title.
E78.G73S37   1990   978'.00497–dc20   89-24829

Book design by Sharon L. Sklar

For information address World Wisdom Books
P. O. Box 2682, Bloomington, Indiana 47402

Printed in Japan

The sacred woman then started to leave the lodge, but turning again to Standing Hollow Horn, she said: "Behold this pipe! Always remember how sacred it is, and treat it as such, for it will take you to the end. Remember, in me there are four ages. I am leaving now, but I shall look back on your people in every age, and at the end I shall return."

—WORDS OF PTE SAN WIN AFTER BRINGING
THE SACRED PIPE TO THE SIOUX

CONTENTS

Contents   viii

PLATES

PUBLISHER'S PREFACE

LONG KNOWN in Europe as one of the foremost authorities on comparative religion and the most eminent spokesman of the *religio perennis,* Frithjof Schuon has had a profound lifelong interest in and affinity with the Plains Indians of North America. During his long career as an author, he has written several articles on the most salient aspects of the Plains Indian tradition, many of which have appeared in the English translations of his books, while at the same time—as a very gifted artist—he has painted scenes of the Plains Indian world throughout his life. In this volume, the two are combined, resulting in a truly insightful vision of the lifeways of a people whose heroism and powerful originality have made them an enduring subject of fascination the world over.

Schuon's knowledge of Indian traditions, however, goes beyond the ordinary scholarly realm. His contact with representatives of Plains Indian spirituality has won him many friends among those seeking to preserve their sacred ways in the face of an ever-encroaching world of white "civilizationism." From meetings in the 1950s with members of the Sioux and Crow tribes visiting Europe, Schuon formed lasting personal ties, most notably with Thomas Yellowtail, who for many years held the function of Sun Dance Chief of the Crows. Schuon and his wife made two extensive journeys in the American West visiting their friends, and the many experiences, impressions and reflections gained on these trips Schuon recorded in a travel diary, excerpts from which (translated from German) appear here. In addition to these writings, excerpts from previously unpublished correspondence are presented which, together with the articles and paintings, offer the reader a unique perspective, "essentialized" in its approach while being at the same time all-embracing and integrally human.

Schuon once wrote: "What one can give to the Indians is strengthening light and what one can receive from them is luminous strength." This volume is intended to cast the strengthening light of the perennial religion on all in the Indian civilization that gives it its grandeur and beauty, its Truth and Holiness.

DEBORAH WILLSEY

INTRODUCTION
BY THOMAS YELLOWTAIL

I AM very pleased to make an introduction for Frithjof Schuon. Our friendship is now more than 36 years old and we have seen each other often during that time. Each time we meet we speak about many different things, but we always talk about traditional Indian religion. Because of these talks, I know how he feels about our way.

When we first met, I was a common man and not well known. Although I was a sun dancer, I was not yet selected to be a medicine man and the Sun Dance Chief of the Crow tribe. Our friendship has always been based on the love we both have for all sacred things and prayer. This is the most important thing for both of us, prayer and the sacred. In this we are in the same boat.

We first met in 1953. In that summer of 36 years ago, my wife and I were members of a group of Crow Indian dancers who toured Europe, North Africa and the Middle East performing traditional Indian dances. On that trip we performed in Paris for several weeks. One day the Schuons introduced themselves to my wife and me in the lobby of our hotel. They explained to us that they had watched our performance for several days and wanted to meet us. We spoke awhile and knew right away that we had much in common. During the next few days in Paris we saw them often and even held a Sun Dance prayer meeting with them in our hotel room. We arranged to meet them later and stay with them at the Schuon home in Switzerland. About a month later our opportunity came and my wife and I spent a week in the Schuon home. That is how we met.

In both 1959 and 1963 the Schuons traveled to the United States to attend the Shoshoni Sun Dance with me and to meet with Indians of many tribes. In 1963 we camped together in Yellowstone Park. I was with Mr. Schuon in Sheridan, Wyoming in 1959 when he was adopted into the Sioux tribe in a ceremony at the All American Indian Days. Each year since 1980 we have come together for a visit. During one of these visits in 1987, I held a ceremony and adopted him as a member of my family. It is better that he is now both a Crow and a Sioux.

Mr. Schuon's paintings are very good. The paintings in this book are only a few of the many paintings he has made. His paintings show the spirit of the olden day Indians. They allow a person to look back and see the old timers in their sacred surroundings. Everything around the olden day Indians reminded them of their sacred center: the nature, the clothing, the tipi and the way of life. This is how it was and how it should be. Because Mr. Schuon knows and loves the spirit of the olden day Indians he can show this spirit in his paintings. This is very good to see. For most readers the paintings will help them understand how these old timers lived. I myself enjoy the paintings very much.

It is a very good thing to see a book with Mr. Schuon's writings about the American Indians. His words are important because he sees the Indian traditional religion with the eyes of a man who prays and who loves the Indians. He has studied all the religions in the world so he can compare our Indian ways to the ways of other religions.

If a reader starts to read a chapter and becomes confused because of some of the difficult words, don't stop or put this book down. Keep reading and you'll come to thoughts that you will understand. Every-one interested in religion can gain something with this book. Anyone who doesn't know the Indians will learn something about how it was in olden days and how it should be. Anyone who already knows something about the Indians will never forget this book. It is certainly an important message.

THOMAS YELLOWTAIL

Wyola, Montana
September 22, 1989

Frithjof Schuon:
Metaphysician and Artist

Frithjof Schuon was born in Basle, Switzerland, on June 18, 1907. His father, a great concert violinist and teacher at the Basle Conservatory of Music, was a native of southern Germany, while his mother came from an Alsatian family. Until the age of thirteen Schuon lived in Basle and attended school there, but the untimely death of his father obliged his mother, for reasons of economy, to return with her two young sons to her family in Mulhouse, France; and thus it was that Schuon received a French-language education in addition to his German one. At sixteen, Schuon left school to become self-supporting as a textile designer—a type of work which made only the most modest demands upon the remarkable artistic talent that he had as yet been given little opportunity to develop. As a child he had already taken much pleasure in drawing and painting, but he never received any formal training in the arts.

As a boy, Schuon had heard much about the Indians from his paternal grandmother, who as a young girl had spent some time in Washington D.C. There she had become personally acquainted with a Sioux member of a delegation of chiefs to the nation's capital, and although she was not allowed to accept his offer of marriage, she never forgot her Indian friend or his people and later transmitted her love and admiration for the Indians to her children and grandchildren.

After painting scenes of Plains Indian life for several years, Schuon finally met and made friends with a number of members of the Crow tribe in Paris, in the winter of 1953. They had come to Europe to give performances under the auspices of Reginald Laubin and his wife, the well-known performers and preservers of traditional American Indian dances. After Paris, several of the group came to Lausanne, Switzerland for a week of vacation between their theatrical engagements, in order to visit the Schuons—notably Thomas Yellowtail, who subsequently became an important medicine man and a leader of the Sun Dance religion. Five years later, the Schuons traveled to Brussels in order to meet a group of sixty Sioux who had come to give Wild West performances in connection with the World's Fair, and with some of whom they developed a lifelong friendship.

These meetings paved the way for the Schuons' first visit to America, in the summer of 1959, when they were warmly welcomed on the Sioux reservations in South Dakota, and the Crow reservation in southern Montana. In the company of Indian friends they visited other tribes of the Plains and had the opportunity to attend a Sun Dance at Fort Hall, Idaho, on the Shoshoni-Bannock reservation. When at Pine Ridge, the Schuons were adopted into the family of Chief James Red Cloud, a grandson of the great chief known to history. The old chief gave Schuon the name of Wambali Ohitika—Brave Eagle—the name of his famous forbear's brother. Later, at an Indian festival in Sheridan, Wyoming, the Schuons were officially received into the Sioux tribe, and Schuon was given the name of Wicahpi Wiyakpa—Bright Star. His wife also received a name from Chief Red Cloud and another at Sheridan, but she gives preference to her first Indian name, Wambali Oyate Win—Eagle People Woman—given to her by old Black Elk, the renowned Sioux medicine man, through the intermediary of their mutual friend Joseph Brown, at the time he was recording Black Elk's explanation of the Sioux rites.*

In 1963, the Schuons visited the Plains tribes a second time, spending the summer among their Indian friends and once again attending a Sun Dance at Fort Hall. During this trip, Schuon took the opportunity to visit the grave of Black Elk in Manderson, South Dakota, and to spend some time with the venerable medicine man's son Benjamin in the Black Hills. He had already met him during his first trip to the West and then again in the fall of 1962 when the Schuons spent several days in his company in Paris.

The artistic works of Frithjof Schuon are oil paintings, whose height and width rarely exceed 24 inches. From a stylistic point of view, they combine the traditional rules of pictorial art with the technique of Western painting. Although traditionalist in his observance of certain elementary principles, Schuon limits himself neither to the style of icons nor to that of Oriental art.

The traditional rules just alluded to are these: to avoid a strict observance of the laws of perspective and to use neither foreshortening nor shading—shading, however, being permitted to the extent that relief in faces and bodies may require, as the example of various icons demonstrates. The fact that Schuon combines these rules with a kind of intellectual rigor on the one hand and an adequate observation of Nature on the other gives to his painting a powerful originality and exceptional expressiveness. In short, he combines the positive features of Western art with the rigor and symbolism of the Egyptian wall

---

* *The Sacred Pipe,* recorded and edited by Joseph Epes Brown, Norman, University of Oklahoma Press, 1953.

painting or the Hindu miniature. Perhaps one could say that Schuon's work, as regards its technical aspects, lies somewhere between the Hindu miniature and expressionism, while at the same time being flavored with a certain influence from Japan.

The artistic side, with Schuon, springs from a consciousness of universal symbolism; for God manifests His Qualities through beauty. There is the beauty of virgin Nature and of man and of art; genuine and legitimate art always has something of the sacred in it, whether directly or indirectly. Man lives by Truth and by Beauty; Schuon writes books and paints pictures. His books express the metaphysical doctrine in which all the religious systems and all the spiritual methods have their origin; he thus takes his stand in the perspective of the *philosophia perennis*. In his paintings, Schuon's intention is to express inward truths, and he does this in a manner that is quite simple, spontaneous and natural, and without any affectation of didactic symbolism. Fundamentally, what he portrays are higher realities as lived through the medium of his own soul, and he does so by means of human portraits and scenes taken for the most part from the life of the Plains Indians. But he has also painted a number of pictures of the Virgin-Mother, not in the style of Christian icons but in the form of the Biblical Shulamite or the Hindu Shakti.

Much of Schuon's intellectual knowledge may be accounted for in terms of his extraordinary aesthetic intuition. It suffices for him to see—in a museum, for example—an object from a traditional civilization, to be able to perceive, through a sort of "chain reaction," a whole ensemble of intellectual, spiritual and psychological principles which operate within that world. An important point in his doctrine is that beauty is not a matter of taste, thus of subjective appreciation, but that, on the contrary, it is an objective and hence obligating reality; the human right to personal affinity—or to "personal selection," if one likes—is altogether independent from aesthetic discrimination, that is to say from the understanding of forms.

Schuon has written in one of his letters: "What I seek to express in my paintings—and indeed I cannot express anything other—is the Sacred combined with Beauty. Thus, spiritual attitudes and virtues of soul. And the vibration that emanates from the paintings must lead inward."

BARBARA PERRY

PART ONE

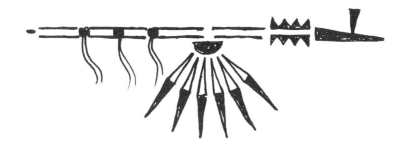

Articles

The Symbolist Mind

According to a very prevalent error —one which has even become more or less "official" in the wake of evolutionism—all traditional symbols were originally understood in a strictly literal sense, and symbolism properly so called only developed as a result of an "intellectual awakening" which took place later. This is an opinion that completely reverses the normal relationship of things, as do all analogous hypotheses arising from an evolutionist context. In reality, what later appears as a superadded meaning was already implicitly present, and the "intellectualization" of symbols is the result, not of an intellectual progress, but on the contrary of a loss, by the majority, of primordial intelligence. It is thus on account of an increasingly defective understanding of symbols and in order to ward off the danger of "idolatry" (and not to escape from a supposedly preexistent, but in fact nonexistent, idolatry) that tradition has felt obliged to verbally explicate symbols which at the origin—the "Divine Age"—were in themselves fully adequate to transmit metaphysical truths.

This error of believing that at the origin everything was "material" and "gross"—wrongly called "concrete"—has even led some to deny at all cost that "primitive" peoples, notably the North American Indians, have the idea of a Supreme God, and they have often sought to do this with the aid of arguments which prove exactly the contrary. What incomprehensions of this sort reveal more than anything, is that scientific "specialization" alone—the knowledge of cranial shapes, languages, puberty rites, culinary methods, and so forth—does not amount to the intellectual qualification enabling one to penetrate ideas and symbols. One example among many others: because the ideas of the North American Indians are not understood (in the absence of the indispensable keys, which are also a part of science, to say the least), these ideas are deemed to be "vague"; or it is said that the "Mystery" of the Indian is not a "Spirit"—"which primitive man is incapable of conceiving, except thanks to the white man's concept and research"[1] —without telling us either what is meant by "Spirit," or why the "Mystery" in question is not one. What possible importance can the "concept of the white man" have for the Indian, and how can the ethnologists know what the Indian thinks apart from the "investigation of the white man"? Indian ideas are reproached for their "protean" character, which is deemed incompatible with the "more differentiated language of civilization."[2] As if the terminology—or specialist jargon—of white men were a criterion of truth or of intellectual value, and as if, for the Indians, what was at stake were mere words, and not truths or experiences![3]

---

1. W. J. McGee, in *The Siouan Indians,* Washington D.C., Smithsonian Institute Bureau of Ethnology, *15th Annual Report,* 1897.

2. Ibid.

3. One author attaches no importance to Indian declarations, made at the beginning of the 19th century, confirming the immemorial existence of the idea of a Supreme Spirit, and to prove that this idea is only an abstraction imported by white men, he quotes the following fact, dating from a time (1701) when the same Indians

The idea that, thanks to an "intellectual awakening" due to "evolution," men finally realized the "grossness" of their tradition and that in order to remedy this, they ingeniously invented explanations that tend, arbitrarily, to lend the images a superior meaning—this idea runs counter not only to the intrinsic truth of the symbolism in question, but also to what is psychologically possible. For if the intellectual elite, or the collective sensibility, finally realized the "grossness"—and thus the falseness[4]—of the myths, the normal reaction would have been to replace them with something better or more "refined," but such a substitution has never taken place anywhere. The maintenance of the tradition can only be explained by its own immutable value, that is to say, by the element of "absoluteness" which it comprises by definition and which renders it inalterable in its essential form. To believe that men would be willing to maintain their tradition for other reasons is one of the most absurd or even most impertinent errors, for it is in fact to underestimate the human species. Neither do we accept the hypothesis of

---

had as yet undergone no white influence: "In the course of the conversation (William) Penn asked one of the Lenape (Delaware) interpreters to explain to him the notion which the Natives had of God. The Indian was embarrassed, and sought in vain for words. Finally he drew a series of concentric circles on the ground, and, indicating their centre, said that this was the place where the Great Man was symbolically situated." (Werner Müller, *Die Relgionen der Waldindianer Nordamerikas*, Berlin, D. Reimer, 1956, the chapter entitled: *"Der Grosse Geist und die Kardinalpunkte."*) One could not furnish a clearer proof of incomprehension than the argument based on this incident, namely that for the Delawares God was a drawing, thus something "concrete" and not an "abstraction"! In the same vein: "The spirit is something without space and without place; to translate *manitu* by this term is all the more improper in that even the most recent sources know the place of *manitu* to be the zenith or sky. That the Cree should seek *manitu* 'somewhere above,' or that the Menomini localize their *mäch häwätuk* in the fourth atmosphere, or that the Fox place their *kechi manetoa* in the Milky Way—all this means only one thing, namely, that the supreme *manitu* has the same sensible character as the *manitus* of lesser importance" (ibid.). The one essential point is entirely missed, namely, why it is that this supreme *manitu* is situated in the sky and not in a cooking pot! When there is ignorance to this degree both as regards symbolism and the symbolist mentality, it would obviously be better not to concern oneself with symbolism at all.

4. For if they were not false, why reproach them for their "grossness"?

"pre-logical" thought[5] because here again it is a question of symbolist thought, which, without ever being illogical, is rather supra-logical in that it transcends the limits of reason, and thus of mental constructions, doubts, conclusions, hypotheses.[6]

It would be quite erroneous to believe that the symbolist mentality consists in selecting from the exterior world images on which to superimpose more or less farfetched meanings; this would be a pastime incompatible with wisdom. On the contrary, the symbolist vision of the cosmos is a priori a spontaneous perspective that bases itself on the essential nature—or the metaphysical transparency—of phenomena, rather than cutting these off from their prototypes. The man of rationalist formation, whose mind is anchored in the material as such, starts from experience and sees things in their existential isolation. Water is for him—when he considers it aside from poetry—a substance composed of oxygen and hydrogen, to which an allegorical significance can be attributed if one wishes, but without there being a necessary ontological connection between the material thing and the idea associated

---

5. Likewise terms such as "prepolydemonism," "polydemonism," "anthropolatry," "theanthropism," and so forth, indicate classifications which are as superficial as they are conjectural. Lévy-Bruhl, who considers that "primitive mentality, as is well known, is above all concrete and not at all conceptual" and that "nothing is more foreign to it than the idea of a one and universal God," attributes to a "pre-logical" outlook the idea that "each plant . . . has its special creator." Now Islam, which is certainly not "pre-logical," teaches that each drop of rain is deposited by an angel; the idea of "guardian angel," incidentally, is not unrelated to the perspective—entirely "logical"—which is in question here. We do not know whether for the Lévy-Bruhl school the pygmies are "primitives," but at all events the existence, on their part, of the idea of a Supreme God is not in doubt (cf. R. P. Trilles, *L'Ame du Pygmée d'Afrique*, Paris, Editions du Cerf, 1945).

6. It is worthwhile also to point out the abuse of the word "magic." Authors who at every turn speak of "magical world-picture" (*magisches Weltbild*) are obviously ignorant of what it is all about, or rather have only a vague notion of the cosmic analogies which magic sets in motion.

PLATE I

with it. The symbolist mind, on the contrary, is intuitive in a superior sense, reasoning and experience having for it the function of an occasional cause only and not of a foundation. The symbolist mind sees appearances in their connection with essences: in its manner of vision, water is primarily the sensible appearance of a principle-reality, a *kami* (Japanese) or a *manitu* (Algonquin) or a *wakan* (Sioux);[7] this means that it sees things, not "superficially" only, but above all "in depth," or that it perceives them in their "participative" or "unitive" dimension as well as in their "separative" dimension. When some ethnologist declares that "there is no *manitu* outside the world of appearances," this simply means that he is unaware that for the symbolist mind appearances do not exist entirely on their own; he is thus unaware of the essential and is wasting his time in concerning himself with symbols. Moreover, this false "concretism"—or this tendency to reduce symbolism, no matter how improbably, to a kind of brute and unintelligible sensualism, indeed a kind of existentialism *avant la lettre*—far from coming closer to Nature or the origins, is in fact a typical reaction of "civilized" man—in the banal and absurd sense of the term; it is the reaction of a brain supersaturated with artificial constructions and sophistry.[8]

And this is important: on the one hand, we do not say that the symbolist thinks "principle" or "idea" when he sees water, fire or

7. As regards these Indian expressions, so needlessly the subject of controversy, we see no reason for not translating them as "spirit," "mystery" or "sacred," depending on the case. It is obviously unreasonable to suppose that these expressions have no meaning, that the Indians speak in order to say nothing, or that they adopt modes of expression without knowing why. That there is no complete equivalence between one language and another—or between one thought and another—is an entirely different question.

8. This is why—be it said in passing—we distrust facile claims to a "primitive purity" or to a "concreteness" that disdains "speculations," hence all these anti-Scholastic reversions to the "simplicity of the Fathers"; for in such cases it is too often a question of mere incapacity, which, instead of admitting what it is, prefers to hide behind the illusion of a superior attitude.

some other phenomenon of Nature; it is simply a question of our making the reader understand what the symbolist "sees," inasmuch as "seeing" and "thinking" are for him synonymous;[9] on the other hand, we do not maintain that every individual belonging to a collectivity of symbolist or contemplative mentality is himself fully conscious of all that the symbols mean, otherwise spontaneous symbolism would not be the prerogative of periods which may be qualified as "primordial," and later commentaries would be without justification. The existence of these commentaries proves precisely a certain enfeeblement by comparison with the "Golden Age," whence the need for a more explicit doctrine, capable of eliminating all sorts of latent errors. For the symbolist mentality, like everything of a collective character, is not proof against decadence: in the consciousness of a given individual or group it may degenerate into a kind of "idolatry,"[10] but then it ceases to be symbolist and becomes something else. To reproach the North American Indians or the Shintoists with having an idolatrous or zoolatrous attitude amounts in short to attributing to them an anti-symbolist mentality, which is contrary to the real facts. For the Indian, the bison is a "divinity"—or a "divine function"—but the very fact that he hunts it proves that he distinguishes clearly between the "real" entity and the "accidental" or "illusory" form.[11] Even supposing that in the case of a

---

9. The opposite is only true in a superior sense, which has no longer any connection with the sensible order. For the metaphysician, to think is to "see" principles or "ideas."

10. Likewise, a metaphysical doctrine can lose its characteristics by degenerating, through successive degrees of incomprehensions to the level of a purely logical—and thus fragmentary and sterile—system. Idolatry in the strict sense of the term is perhaps primarily a Semitic phenomenon; with the ancient Arabs it did not even have the excuse of deriving from a symbolism, for their idols frequently had purely human and empirical origins.

11. Similarly, according to the testimony of a Sioux at the end of the 19th century: "The Red Man divided mind into two parts: the spiritual mind and the physical mind. The first is pure spirit, concerned only with the essence of things, and it was this he sought to strengthen by spiritual prayer, during which the body is subdued

particular symbolist there is an element of "pantheism," his error would be no greater than that of the "monotheist" for whom things are nothing but themselves, and for whom the symbolism is merely a superadded allegory. The whole question is to know which of the two errors is most opportune or the least harmful for a given mentality; consequently we can even go so far as to say that an idolatrous attitude on the part of a Hindu or a Far-Easterner will not have the same psychological import as on the part of a Semite or European.

Primordial man sees the "greater" in the "lesser": the world of Nature, in fact, reflects Heaven, and conveys, in an existential language, a divine message that is at once multiple and unique. The moral result of this perspective of the "translucid" cosmos is a respectful and even devotional attitude towards virgin Nature, this sanctuary—the key to which has been lost to the West since the disappearance of the mythologies—which fortifies and inspires those of its children who have retained the sense of its mysteries, as Terra did for Antheia. Christianity, having had to react against a truly "pagan" spirit (in the Biblical sense of "idolatrous") has at the same time caused to disappear—as always happens in such cases—values which did not deserve the reproach of paganism; having to oppose, among the Mediterraneans, a philosophic and "flat" "naturalism," it suppressed at the same time, above all in the Nordics, a "naturism" of a spiritual character.[12] Modern technology is the result—quite indirect, no doubt—of a perspective which, having banished from Nature the gods and the

---

by fasting and hardships. In this type of prayer there was no beseeching of favor or help. All matters of personal or selfish concern, as success in hunting or warfare, relief from sickness, or the sparing of a beloved life, were definitely relegated to the plane of the lower or material mind, and all ceremonies, charms or incantations designed to secure a benefit or to avert a danger, were recognized as emanating from the physical self." See Charles A. Eastman (Ohiyesa), *The Soul of the Indian*, Lincoln, University of Nebraska Press, 1980.

12. An echo of this, as it were, is to be found in the *Poverello* of Assisi.

genies, and having also by this very fact rendered it profane,[13] has ended by allowing it to be "profaned" in the most brutal sense of the word. The Promethean Westerner—but not every Westerner—is affected by a kind of innate contempt for Nature: for him Nature is a property to be enjoyed or exploited,[14] or even an enemy to be conquered; it is not a "property of the Gods" as in Bali, but a "raw material" doomed to industrial or sentimental exploitation, according to

---

13. It must be said that the Greeks of the classical period, with their scientific empiricism, were the first to deprive Nature of her majesty, without, for all that, dethroning her in the popular consciousness. There were certainly Dodona and other sanctuaries under the open sky, but it must not be forgotten that the ancient temple is opposed to virgin Nature as order is opposed to chaos, or reason to dream. Obviously this is also true, to a certain extent and by the nature of things, of all human art, but the Greco-Roman mind is peculiar in being much more attached to the idea of "perfection" than to that of the "infinite"; "perfection" or "order" becomes the very content of its art, to the point of excluding from it all remembrance of the Essences.— Doubtless this partial truth ought to be complemented by another, this time positive in character: a friend once remarked, quite rightly, that the God of the Greeks, who is a "geometrician," did not "create," but "measured" the world, as light "measures" space. Thus the Greek temple, with its clarity, its straight lines, its precise rhythms, incarnates or rather "crystallizes" light, and in this respect it is opposed, not to Nature as such, but to the earth, thus to matter, weight, opacity. In other words, it does not merely constitute an abstract and limitative systematization, but also a revelation of the Intellect and a totality. The same remark could also be made about the Taj Mahal and other Islamic buildings of the kind, but with this difference, that in the latter cases luminosity is conceived in a less "mathematical" manner, and one which is also much nearer to the idea of the Infinite.

14. For Christian theology, Nature's only purpose seems to be to serve earthly man—one could ask of what service to him a particular pachyderm of the tropics or a sea monster is—so much so that the Heavenly Jerusalem, where man no longer has any physical needs, contains no animals or plants; contrary to Moslem symbolism, it is a paradise of crystal. The *jannāt* of Islam, it is true, are "made of pearl, ruby and emerald," but they are nevertheless gardens containing trees, fruits, flowers, birds. There is no question here of criticizing any symbolism—that goes without saying —but only certain speculations which are derived from it. Thus, it has been held that the soul of the animal exists only through matter, of which it is no more than the interior reflection; but this leaves unexplained, firstly the differences of form—qualitative and psychological—among the animals, and then the affective, and even contemplative, traits which they manifest. When the Bible says that man must rule over the animals, it seems to us that this does not imply that they are only there to serve him.

taste and circumstances.[15] This dethronement of Nature, or this scission between man and the earth—a reflection of the scission between man and Heaven—has borne such bitter fruits that it should not be difficult to admit that, in these days, the timeless message of Nature constitutes a spiritual viaticum of the first importance. Some may object that the West has always had—especially in the 18th and 19th centuries—its returns to virgin Nature, but this is not what we mean, since we have no use for a romantic and "deist," or even atheistic "naturism."[16] It is not a question of projecting a supersaturated and disillusioned individualism into a desecrated Nature—this would be a worldliness like any other—but, on the contrary, of rediscovering in Nature, on the basis of the traditional outlook, the divine substance which is inherent in it; in other words, to "see God everywhere," and to see nothing apart from His mysterious presence.

---

15. One readily talks about "conquering" the Matterhorn, Everest, Annapurna, the Indus, the moon, space, and so forth. In practice Nature is simply the opponent to be struck down: the world is divided into two camps, human beings and Nature. To be sure, there is a certain amount of truth in this, but everything depends on the meaning given to this opposition.

16. It is essential not to confuse symbolism and "naturism," as we understand them, with the philosophic and literary movements which abusively lay claim to these terms. Nothing is further from Vedic, Shintoist or North American symbolism than the artistic naturalism of the Greco-Romans and their anecdotal interpretation of the myths.

A Metaphysic of Virgin Nature

The whole tradition of the Indians of North America, excepting those of the Northwest, California and some of the Southwest, is contained in the cross inscribed in the circle, from the viewpoint of geometric symbolism: the circle corresponds to the Sky, while the cross marks the Four Directions of space and all the other quaternaries of the Universe; it also marks the vertical ternary Earth-Man-Sky, which puts the horizontal quaternary on three levels. It could moreover be said that the wisdom of the Red Indians is based, symbolically speaking, on the "Pythagorean" numbers four and three—the first being "horizontal" and the second "vertical"—and on their combination, the number twelve. This "duodecimality" should be pictured as composed of three horizontal quaternaries placed one above another on a central axis, or more precisely of three disks upon each of which is the horizontal cross of the four directions. These three degrees are sometimes represented in the form of three rings painted on the Sun Dance tree.[1]

---

1. Joseph Epes Brown, known for his study on the sacred pipe, once wrote us concerning a Crow shaman: "He explained to me with perfect clarity the metaphysic

In the symbolism of the cross and the circle, the spatial and static circle of the earth combines with the dynamic and temporal circle of the day or the sky: the circle can either be the horizon with—assuming the cross therein—the four cardinal points, or it can be the course of the sun with the morning, the day, the evening and the night, or the year with the spring, the summer, the autumn and the winter.

And this is important: man is the center, both of the four horizontal directions of space, and of the vertical ternary of the cosmic hierarchy; in this latter respect, he is identified with Life and is mediator between the Earth "under his feet" and the Sky "over his head,"[2] or between inertia and light. In the first respect he is the Intelligence in which the four quarters are reflected and united, and he is thus identified with the cosmic axis, the world tree. He is the Calumet which unites all beings in a single prayer, while again, he is the central Fire which marks the middle of the world, and still again (which comes to the same thing) he is the ember in the Calumet that transmutes the tobacco into smoke or Earth into Sky. Man is thus twice "in the middle," first on the horizontal plane as Intelligence and spokesman for all terrestrial creatures (fragmentary in relation to him), and secondly, on

---

of the Sun Dance, telling me among other things that the lodge represents the Universe: the tree of life at the center is its axis, whose branches reach upwards, beyond the Universe to the Infinite. There are three rings painted on the trunk, which represent the three worlds: the body, the soul, the spirit, or the 'gross,' the 'subtle' and the 'pure.' The axis is everywhere and consequently passes through each being; the ultimate aim of the dance is to withdraw from the periphery—after purification, sacrifice and other rites—and to approach the center, in order to become identified with it."

2. Hartley Burr Alexander remarks (in *The World's Rim*, Lincoln, Nebraska, University of Nebraska Press, 1953) that man is said upon waking up in the morning to look instinctively towards the dawning light which dispels the darkness, hence towards the east, and that this direction (in which a number of Indian rites begin and towards which the tents and lodges open) will accordingly be "front" for him. West will be "behind," south "to the right," and north "to the left." Moreover the sensible world for a man standing (and this is his natural position that distinguishes him from the quadrupeds) is divided into three spheres, likewise found in the structure of the human body: the ground under his feet, the sky over his head—or feet and head—and the middle of the body, the navel or region of the womb, symbol of life.

the vertical axis, as mediator: in him Earth and Sky meet, and in him are synthesized the essential possibilities on his plane of existence.

If the human head corresponds to the Sky and the feet represent the Earth, the region of the navel or the womb stands for Man. Man is spirit incarnate;[3] if he were only matter, he would be identified with the feet; if he were only spirit, he would be the head, that is, the Sky; he would be the Great Spirit. But the object of his existence is to be in the middle: it is to transcend matter while being situated there, and to realize the light, the Sky, starting from this intermediary level. It is true that the other creatures also participate in life, but man synthesizes them: he carries all life within himself and thus becomes the spokesman for all life, the vertical axis where life opens onto the spirit and where it becomes spirit. In all terrestrial creatures the cold inertia of matter becomes heat, but in man alone does heat become light.

We said that the lower creatures are fragmentary; but they do not have only this "accidental" aspect which allows man to kill them and use them for nourishment, they also have an "essential" aspect due to their concrete symbolism on the one hand and their "anteriority" on the other: created before man, they can manifest something of the Divine Origin, and it is this aspect which sometimes calls for their veneration; it is by virtue of this transcendent aspect that the Great Spirit readily manifests Itself—in the world of the Indians—through animals and plants, and even through the great phenomena of Nature, such as the sun, the rock, the sky, or the earth.[4] The multiple manifestation of

---

3. Let us recall here this formula: *Et benedictus fructus ventris tui. . . .* Terrestrial man lives in the womb of the macrocosm and not in its celestial head.

4. The son of the Sioux holy man Black Elk (cf. John Neihardt's *Black Elk Speaks*, New York, Washington Square Press, 1972 and Joseph Epes Brown's *The Sacred Pipe*, Lincoln, University of Nebraska Press, 1953) stressed to us that the Indians do not worship the rocks, trees and animals; but because man was created only after all other creatures, it is through them that he can and must approach God. The following words of another Sioux (spoken as we passed with him near the spurs of the Black Hills) show the same veneration for nature: "This is the Buffalo Gap. It was

PLATE II

the Great Spirit, from the viewpoint of symbolism and celestial action, is the equivalent of the Great Spirit; things are not mysteries in themselves, but manifestations of mysteries, and the Great Spirit, or the Great Mystery,[5] synthesizes them in Its transcendent Unity.

$$\mathbf{\supset\supset\supset}$$

An original feature of the Indian tradition is that the "prophetic" element, which elsewhere crystallizes in rare *avatāras*, is spread out so to speak over all the members of the tribes, without for that abolishing the differences in degrees and the crucial manifestations. In a certain sense, however surprising as it may seem, each man is his own prophet having received his own revelation, though naturally within the framework of the tradition in general, which strictly regulates the outward and even inward modalities of this collective prophethood. But let us repeat, this could never prevent the existence of major revelations valid for a particular tribal collectivity, or for all, as with the Calumet and the Sun Dance. The Indian's apparent "individualism" is explained by the spiritual role of man as such, of the free and qualitative person, of deed and character; it is also prompted by the relationship between the individual and the tribe, by a reciprocity of gift, of duty, of generosity. But the essential in this social context is fidelity to

---

through this door that the buffalo herds used to come streaming in. Just as the Great Spirit has made a Door through which man can come to Him, so has He made a door through which the buffaloes come to man." The buffalo is not only a gift from God for the sustenance of man, it is also a symbol of the Divine Word and an instrument of Revelation. The Calumet was brought by the White Buffalo Woman, a heavenly buffalo transformed into a woman. "Our tradition," an old Cheyenne told us, "is the same as the one in the Bible; God is invisible, He is pure Spirit. The sun and the earth are not God, but for us they are something like father and mother."

5. There are Indian languages in which the Divine Spirit is designated in a totally different way, where for example one speaks of the "Great Solar Power," but the fundamental doctrine remains the same.

oneself, to one's own vision, one's own pact with a particular theophany, or in other terms, with one's own "medicine" or one's own "totem."[6]

Another feature characteristic of the Indian, which seems in contradiction with the preceding one, is his "polysynthesism," namely his consciousness of the profound homogeneity of the created world and the sense of universal solidarity which results therefrom. All creatures, including plants and even minerals—and likewise things in Nature, such as stars or wind—are brothers; everything is animate, and each thing depends in a certain manner on all the others. Man, while mediator in a determinate respect, is not opposed, in another respect, to the rest of creation. The Indian like all the yellow race—for he is a Mongoloid—stays in Nature and is never detached from it; psychologically he is like a samurai become hunter or nomad; his contemplativeness, where it is most intimate and exalted, is without doubt not unrelated to that intuitive and inarticulate method which is Zen, or in other respects, to the spiritualized Nature in Shinto.

In the wisdoms of the Old World, what perhaps most adequately—and also most profoundly—expresses the spiritual attitude of the "eternal Red Indian" is the *Bhagavad Gītā*. Combat is a *modus vivendi*—willed by Nature—on which is superimposed a silent and impassible contemplation in virgin solitude; in the teaching of Krishna there is a combative, but detached, engagement in the current of forms, and at the same time a contemplation which stays in the center, with the incorruptibility of rock. This is not how the Indians have always been in fact— no civilization has ever been able to realize integrally its "ideal"—

---

6. This word, which has become conventional in the language of the whites, derives from the Ojibway *ototeman*, "his brother-sister kin." The totemistic animal is not lacking analogy with our "guardian angel"; moreover, let us not forget that the Holy Spirit in the Gospels did not disdain to appear in the form of a dove, and that it is the apparition of a miraculous stag which converted St. Hubert.

but how their tradition would have them be, and how they have been as regards their elect and in their finest moments, if one may put it thus.

The Red Indian tradition is often reproached with having an inadequate conception of the next world. But this apparent lack has here the same reasons as in the similar case of Shintoism: in these perspectives the need for an elaborated eschatology does not make itself felt, for the hereafter is guaranteed by the as it were obligatory and inevitable quality of this life; this is what explains in both traditions their rigidity as regards doctrine, virtues, code of honor and sense of duty. Also, it must not be overlooked that from the Hindu and Buddhist viewpoint the eschatology of the Semites is likewise relatively incomplete, since it seems to accept on the one hand the idea of a quasi-absolute punishment for an act which is necessarily relative, and on the other hand that of an eternity which has had a beginning. Yet here, as in the case of the Indian and Shintoist eschatologies, we will say that Heaven not only has reasons for speaking, but can also have reasons for keeping silent, according to what the nature of the human receptacle requires.

The traditional Indian was one of the freest men that can be imagined, and at the same time one of the most bound: the vast prairie, the forests and the mountains belonged to him; practically speaking, his vital space knew no limits; yet at no moment could he depart from his religious universe and the role which this imposed upon him. On the one hand he was enclosed within a space that was strictly symbolical—as though his credo had crystallized spatially around him—and on the other he was identified with the implacable course of that great trial which is life; whether in time or in space, the Indian never left the visible symbol, which he acted out and lived; it could be said that he underwent and realized it simultaneously. And it is from this combination of heroic liberty and divine constraint that he derives his fascinating originality and this part-warrior, part-sacerdotal grandeur which—along with other factors, such as the cult of silence and impassibilty—relates him to the Zen samurai of ancient Japan.

The Shamanism of the Red Indians

The word "Shamanism" is used here to mean the traditions of pre-historic origin that are associated with Mongoloid peoples, including the American Indians.[1] In Asia, Shamanism properly so called is met with not only in Siberia, but also in Tibet (in the form of Bön-Po) and in Mongolia, Manchuria and Korea. The pre-Buddhist Chinese tradition, with its Confucian and Taoist branches, is attached to the same traditional family, and the same applies to Japan, where Shamanism has given rise to the specifically Japanese Shinto tradition. Characteristic of all these doctrines is a complementary opposition of Heaven and Earth, and a cult of Nature, the latter being envisaged under the aspect of its essential causality and not of its existential accidentality; they are

---

1. But not the Mexicans and Peruvians, who represent later traditional filiations, such as are sometimes called "Atlantean," and who therefore no longer spring from the eyrie of the "Thunderbird."

also distinguished by a certain parsimony in their eschatology—very apparent even in Confucianism—and above all by the central function of the shaman, assumed in China by the *Tao-tse*[2] and in Tibet by the lamas concerned with divination and exorcism.[3] China and Japan have been mentioned here, not in order that their native traditions should simply be assimilated to Siberian Shamanism, but in order to indicate the place they occupy in relation to the primitive tradition of the yellow race, a tradition of which Shamanism is the most direct and also, it must be admitted, the most uneven and the most ambiguous continuation. These last words suggest the need for some enquiry into the spiritual value of the Siberian and American forms of Shamanism. The general impression is one of the very widest differences of level, but one thing is certain, and it is that among the Red Indians, to whom attention will hereafter be confined, something primordial and pure has been preserved, despite all the obscurations that may have been superimposed on it in certain tribes, perhaps mostly in relatively recent times.

Documents bearing testimony to the spiritual quality of the Red Indians are numerous. A white man who was captured by them in his early infancy at the beginning of the nineteenth century, and who lived until his twentieth year among tribes (Kickapoo, Kansas, Omaha, Osage) who had never had the least contact with a missionary says: "It is certain however that they acknowledge, at least so far as my acquaintance extends, one supreme, all powerful and intelligent Being, viz., the Great Spirit, or the Giver of Life, who created and governs all things. They believe in general that, after the hunting grounds had been formed and supplied with game, he created the first red man and woman, who were very large in their stature, and lived to an exceed-

---

2. Not to be confused with the *Tao-shi,* who are contemplative monks.

3. The line of demarcation between Bön-Po and Lamaism is not always clear, each tradition having influenced the other.

ing old age; that he often held councils and smoked with them, gave them laws to be obeyed and taught them how to take game and cultivate corn: but that in consequence of their disobedience, he withdrew from and abandoned them to the vexations of the Bad Spirit, who had since been instrumental to all their degeneracy and sufferings. They believe him of too exalted a character to be directly the author of evil, and that, notwithstanding the offences of his red children, he continues to shower down on them all the blessings they enjoy; in consequence of this parental regard for them, they are truly filial and sincere in their devotions, and pray to him for such things as they need, and return thanks for such good things as they receive. . . . In all the tribes I have visited, the belief in a future state of existence, and in future rewards and punishments is prevalent. . . . This belief in their accountability to the Great Spirit makes the Indians generally scrupulous and enthusiastic observers of all their traditionary, tuitive, and exemplary dogmas; and it is a fact worthy of remark that neither frigidity, indifference, nor hypocrisy in regard to sacred things, is known to exist among them."[4]

Another testimony, deriving this time from a Christian source, runs as follows: "Belief in a Supreme Being is firmly rooted in the culture of the Chippewas. This Being, called *Kiche Manito*, or Great Spirit, was far removed from them. Prayers were rarely addressed directly to him alone and sacrifices were only offered to him at the feast of the Midewiwin initiates. My informants spoke of him in a tone of submission and extreme reverence. 'He has placed all things on earth and takes care of everything,' added an old man, the most powerful medicine-man of the Short Ear Lake Reservation. One old woman of the same Reservation stated that when praying the ancient Indians first of all addressed *Kiche Manito* and afterwards the other great spirits, the

---

4. John D. Hunter, *Manners and Customs of Several Indian Tribes West of the Mississippi*, republished, Minneapolis, Ross & Haines, 1957.

Kitchi Manito who live in the winds, the snow, the thunder, the tempest, the trees, and in all things. One aged Shaman called Vermilion was convinced that 'all the Indians in his country knew God long before the White men came there; but they did not ask Him for particular things as they do now that they have become Christians. They expected favours from their own special protectors.' Less powerful than *Kiche Manito* were the divinities inhabiting Nature and also the guardian spirits. The belief of the Chippewas in a life after death is made plain by their burial and mourning customs; but they have a tradition that souls after death go towards the West 'where the sun sets,' or 'towards the prairies where are situated the camping-grounds of blessing and eternal happiness.'"[5]

The writer's point of view not being compatible with evolutionism, to say the least of it, the reader will not find in these pages any suggestion of a belief in a crude and pluralistic origin of religions, nor any reason for casting doubt on the "monotheistic" aspect of the tradition of the Indians,[6] more especially because polytheism pure and simple is never anything but a degeneration, and therefore a relatively late phenomenon, and in any case much less widespread than is ordinarily supposed. Primordial monotheism has nothing specifically Semitic about it and is best described as a "pan-monotheism"; otherwise, polytheism could not have been derived from it. This monotheism subsists, or has left some traces, among peoples of the most diverse kind, including the Pygmies of Africa. In the Americas, the Fuegians, for instance, know but a single God dwelling beyond the stars; he has no

---

5. Sister M. Inez Hilger, *Chippewa Child Life and its Cultural Background,* Washington, 1951.

6. In 1770 a woman visionary announced to the Ogalala Sioux that the Great Spirit was angry with them; in the pictographic narratives ("winter counts") of the Ogalala, that year was given the name *Wakan Tanka Knashkiyan* ("Great Spirit in anger"). This happened at a time when the Sioux could not have come under the influence of white monotheism.

body and does not sleep; the stars are his eyes; he has always been and will never die; he has created the world and given to men rules of action. Among the Indians of North America, both those of the Plains and of the Forests, the divine Unity is no doubt less exclusively affirmed and in some cases even seems to be veiled; nevertheless among these peoples nothing is to be found strictly comparable to the anthropomorphic polytheism of the ancient Europeans. It is true that there are several "Great Powers,"[7] but these Powers are either subordinated to a supreme Power which resembles Brahma much more nearly than Jupiter, or they are regarded as a totality or as a supernatural Substance of which we ourselves are parts, as a Sioux explained to the writer. In order to understand this last point, which would represent pantheism if it were taken as a full statement of the concept in question, one must know that ideas concerning the Great Spirit are attached either to the "discontinuous" reality of the Essence, which implies a transcendentalism,[8] or to the "continuous" reality of Substance, which implies a panentheism; nevertheless in the consciousness of the Red Indians the relation of Substance has more importance than that of Essence. One sometimes hears of a magical power animating all things, including man, called *Manito* (Algonquin) or *Orenda* (Iroquois); this power is coagulated or personified, according to the case, in things and beings, including those that belong to the invisible and animic world; it also becomes crystallized in connection with some human subject, as a

---

7. The name *Wakan-Tanka,* literally "Great Sacred" (*wakan* = sacred) is commonly translated "Great Spirit" or "Great Mystery," and has also been rendered as "Great Powers," the plural being justified in view of the polysynthetic significance of the concept.

8. It goes without saying that this word must be understood in its proper sense, and that it has no connection with the Emersonian philosophy to which it lends its name. One might wonder, it may be said in passing, whether Emerson's works do not reveal, in addition to his German idealism, a certain influence coming from the Red Indians.

PLATE III

"totem" or "guardian angel" (the *orayon* of the Iroquois).[9] All this is correct, but with the reservation that the word "magic" which is sometimes used in this connection is far too limitative, and is even erroneous in the sense that it defines a cause in terms of a partial effect. However that may be, the important thing to remember is that the Red Indian theism, while it is not a pluralism of the Mediterranean and "pagan" type, does not correspond exactly to the Abrahamic monotheism either; it is more in the nature of a somewhat "fluid" theosophy—there being no sacred Scripture—akin to Vedic and Far-Eastern conceptions. It is also important to note the emphasis on the aspects of "life" and "power" in the Red Indian outlook, which is very characteristic of a warlike and more or less nomadic mentality.

Certain tribes, especially the Algonquins and Iroquois, make a distinction between the demiurge and the supreme Spirit; the former often assumes a role that borders on the burlesque, or even on the luciferian. Such a conception of the creative Power, and of the primordial dispenser of the arts, is far from being confined to the Red Indians, as is proved, to choose one example only, by the mythologies of the Ancient World where the misdeeds of the Titans stand side by side with those of the gods. In Biblical terms, it can be said that there is no terrestrial Paradise without its serpent, and that without the serpent there can be no fall and therefore no human drama, nor any reconciliation with Heaven. The creation being in any case something that stands apart from God, a deifugal tendency must necessarily be inherent in it, so much so that it can be considered under two aspects, the one divine and the other demiurgic or luciferian. The Red Indians mingle these two aspects, nor are they alone in doing so: one need only recall the case of the god Susano-o in Japanese mythology, the turbulent genius of sea and storm. In short, the demiurge (called *Nanabozho*,

---

9. This is on the whole equivalent to the *Kami* of Shintoism.

Mishabozho and *Napi* by the Algonquins, and *Tharonhiawagon* by the Iroquois) is none other than *Māyā,* the protean principle that combines both the creative Power and the world itself, and is *natura naturans* as well as *natura naturata. Māyā* is beyond good and evil, it expresses both plenitude and privation, the divine and the all too human, and even the titanic and the demonic; sentimental moralism finds it difficult to understand an ambiguity of that order.

So far as cosmogony is concerned, the Red Indian does not really envisage a *creatio ex nihilo,* but rather a sort of transformation. In a celestial world situated above the visible sky there lived in the beginning semi-divine beings, the prototypic and normative personages whom earthly man has to imitate in all things. That heavenly world knew only peace; but a time came when some of these beings sowed the seeds of discord, and then occurred the great change: they were banished to earth and became the ancestors of all earthly creatures. Some, however, were able to remain in Heaven, and these are the geniuses of every essential activity, such as hunting, war, love, cultivation. Consequently, what we call "creation" is, according to the Indians, a change of state or a descent: this is an "emanationist" point of view in the positive and legitimate sense of the word and can be explained here in terms of the predominance, with the Indians, of the idea of Substance, that is to say of a "non-discontinuous" Reality. The image is that of a spiral or star, and not one of concentric circles that are discontinuous in relation to the center, although this second conception must never be lost sight of: the two images are complementary, but the accent is sometimes on the one and sometimes on the other.

What is the precise meaning in concrete terms of this Red Indian idea that everything is "animated"? It means, in principle and metaphysically, that, whatever be the object envisaged, there springs from its existential center an ontological ray, made up of "being," "consciousness" and "life," whereby the object in question is attached, through its subtle or animic root, to its luminous and celestial prototype; from this it follows that in principle it is possible for us to attain the heavenly Essences by taking any thing whatever as starting point. Things are coagulations of universal Substance, while Substance—and this is crucial—is not affected by those accidents in the slightest degree. Substance is not things, but things are it, and they are so by virtue of their existence and their qualities; this is the inner meaning of the polysynthetic animism of the Red Indians, and it is this acute consciousness of the homogeneity of the world of phenomena that explains their spiritual naturism, and also their refusal to detach themselves from Nature and to become engaged in a civilization made up of artifices and servitudes, and carrying within itself the seeds of petrification as well as of corruption. In the view of the Red Indian, as in that of Far-Eastern peoples, the human is situated within Nature and not outside it.

The most eminent manifestations of the Great Spirit are the cardinal points together with the Zenith and Nadir, or with Heaven and Earth, and next in order are such forms as the Sun, the Morning Star, the Rock, the Eagle, the Bison. All these manifestations are within ourselves even though their roots subsist in Divinity. Although the Great Spirit is One, it comprises in itself all those qualities the traces of which we see and the effects of which we experience in the world of appearances. [10]

---

10. Sages among the Indians are by no means ignorant of the contingent and illusory character of the cosmos: "I saw more than I can tell and I understood more than I saw; for I was seeing in a sacred manner the shapes of all things in the spirit, and the shape of all shapes as they must live together like one being." "Crazy Horse dreamed and went into the world where there is nothing but the spirits of all things. That is the real world that is behind this one, and everything we see here is something like a shadow from that world." "I knew the real was yonder and the darkened dream of it was here." (Hehaka Sapa, from *Black Elk Speaks, Being the Life Story of a Holy Man of the Oglala Sioux*, as told through John G. Neihardt, New York, Washington Square Press, 1972.)

The East is Light and Knowledge, and also Peace; the South is Warmth and Life, therefore also Growth and Happiness; the West is fertilizing Water and also Revelation speaking in lightning and thunder; the North is Cold and Purity, or Strength. Thus it is that the Universe, at whatever level it may be considered, whether of Earth, Man or Heaven, is dependent on the four primordial determinations: Light, Heat, Water, Cold. The assigning of qualities in this way to the cardinal points is remarkable because they do not expressly symbolize either the four elements, air, fire, water, earth or their corresponding physical states, dryness, heat, moisture, cold, but rather tend to mix or combine the two sets of four unequally. Thus, North and South are respectively characterized by cold and heat but they do not represent the elements earth and fire, whereas the West corresponds at the same time both to moisture and to water. The East represents drought and above all light, but not air. This asymmetry can be explained as follows: the elements air and earth are respectively identified, in the spatial symbolism of the Universe, with Heaven and Earth, whereas fire, considered as a sacrificial and transmuting element, occupies the Center of all things. If one takes account of the fact that Heaven synthesizes all the active aspects of both quaternaries, that of the elements (air, fire, water, earth) and that of the physical states (drought, heat, moisture, cold), and that Earth synthesizes their passive aspects, it will be seen that the symbolical definitions of the four quarters are intended as a synthesis of both poles, the one heavenly and the other earthly; the North-South axis is earthly and the East-West axis is heavenly.

The factor that is common to all the Red Indians is the fourfold polarity of the cosmic qualities, but the descriptive symbolism can vary from one group to another and especially between groups as different as the Sioux and the Iroquois. Among the Cherokees, for instance, who belong to the latter family, East, South, West, North mean respectively success, happiness, death, adversity, and are represented by the colors red, white, black and blue; whereas among the Sioux all the cardinal points bear a positive meaning, their colors—in the same order of succession—being red, yellow, black and white. However, there is evidently a relationship between North-adversity and North-purification, since trials purify and strengthen, or between West-death and West-revelation since both ideas are related to the beyond. Lastly, with the Ojibway, who belong to the Algonquin group, East is white like the light, South green like vegetation, West red or yellow like the setting sun and North black like the night. The attributions differ with the different points of view, but the fundamental symbolism with its fourfold structure and its polarities is not affected.

The crucial part played by the directions of space in the rite of the Calumet or Sacred Pipe is well known. This rite is the Indian's prayer, in which he speaks not only on his own behalf but also on behalf of all other creatures; the entire Universe prays together with the man who offers the Pipe to the Powers, or to *the* Power.

Mention must also be made here of the other great rites of North American Shamanism: the Sweat Lodge, Solitary Invocation and the Sun Dance;[11] together with that of the Pipe they make up the four principal rites. We have chosen the number four, not as marking any set limit, but because this number is sacred to the Red Indians, and also because it permits of establishing a synthesis that has nothing arbitrary about it.

The "Sweat Lodge" is the chief purificatory rite of the Indians; by its means man is cleansed and becomes a new being. This rite and that of the Pipe are absolutely fundamental; the one that follows is so as well, but in a rather different sense.

Solitary Invocation or "lamenting" or "sending forth a voice" is the most exalted form of prayer; it can be offered silently,[12] as circumstances

---

11. Other rites are more social in their scope.

12. Cf. René Guénon: *"Silence et Solitude,"* in *Etudes Traditionnelles*, March, 1949.

dictate. It is a real spiritual retreat, through which every Indian has to pass once in his youth, with a particular intention, but which he may repeat at any time, according to his inspiration or to circumstances.

The Sun Dance is, in a sense, the prayer of the whole community; to those who take part in it this dance means, esoterically at least, their virtual union with the Solar Spirit, and thus with the Great Spirit. The Sun Dance symbolizes the attachment of the soul to God: just as the dancer is attached to the central tree by thongs that symbolize the sun's rays, so man is attached to Heaven by a mysterious bond which the Indian formerly sealed with his own blood; now it is usual for him simply to keep uninterrupted fast for three or four days. The dancer in this rite is like an eagle flying towards the sun: from a whistle made of eagle's bone he produces a shrill and plaintive sound while imitating the eagle's flight after a fashion, using feathers he carries in his hands. This as it were sacramental relationship with the sun leaves an ineffaceable mark on the soul.[13]

As regards the magical practices of the shamans, one has to distinguish ordinary magic from what might be termed cosmic magic: the latter operates in virtue of the analogies between symbols and their prototypes. Everywhere in Nature, which includes man himself, one meets with like possibilities, substances, forms and movements which correspond to one another qualitatively or typologically; now, the shaman aims at mastering phenomena which by their nature or by accident lie outside his control by using other phenomena of an analogous (and therefore metaphysically "identical") kind which he creates

13. All these rites have been described by Hehaka Sapa in *The Sacred Pipe* recorded and edited by Joseph Epes Brown, Norman, University of Oklahoma Press, 1953.

himself and which are therefore within his sphere of activity. The medicine man may wish to bring rain, to stop a snowstorm, to bring a herd of bison or to cure an illness, and for this purpose he makes use of forms, colors, rhythms, incantations and wordless melodies. All this, however, would be insufficient but for the extraordinary power of concentration of the shaman, acquired as it is through a long training carried out in solitude and silence and in contact with virgin Nature.[14] Concentration can also be acquired thanks to an exceptional gift and through the intervention of a celestial influence.[15]

Behind every sensible phenomenon there lies in fact a reality of an animic order that is independent of the limitations of space and time; it is by getting into touch with these realities, or these subtle and suprasensorial roots of things, that a shaman is able to influence natural phenomena or to foretell the future. All this may sound strange, to say the least of it, to a modern reader whose imagination now bears different imprints and responds to different reflexes than did that of medieval or archaic man; his subconscious, it must be avowed, is warped by a mass of prejudices having intellectual or scientific pretensions. Without going into details, one need only recall, in the words of Shakespeare, that "there are more things in heaven and earth than are dreamt of in your philosophy."

But the shamans are also, and even more particularly, expert magicians in the ordinary sense; their science works with forces of a psychic or animic order, whether individualized or otherwise; it does not introduce, as in the case of cosmic magic, analogies between the microcosm and the macrocosm, or between the various natural reverberations of one and the same "idea." In "white magic," which is normally that of the shamans, the forces called into play, as well as the purpose of the

---

14. A Shoshoni told the writer that since the medicine men have lived in houses they have become impure and lost much of their power.

15. As in the case of Hehaka Sapa.

operation, are either beneficent or else simply neutral. In cases, however, where the spirits are maleficent and where the purpose is equally so, "black magic" or sorcery is involved; in such a case, nothing is done "in God's name," and the link with the higher powers is broken. It goes without saying that practices socially so dangerous or so pernicious in themselves were strictly prohibited among the Red Indians as with other peoples;[16] this does not mean, however, that these practices did not undergo in the case of certain forest tribes, as they did in Europe at the end of the Middle Ages, something like an epidemic expansion, in conformity with their sinister and contagious nature.[17]

One problem that has troubled all who take an interest in the spirituality of the Red Indians is that of the "Ghost Dance" which played so tragic a part in their final defeat. Contrary to current opinion, this dance was not an entirely unprecedented occurrence; several similar movements had arisen long before Wovoka, the originator of the Ghost Dance. In fact, among the tribes of the West the following phenomenon has occurred fairly often: a visionary, who is not necessarily a shaman, undergoes an experience of death and, on coming back to life, brings a message from the beyond in the form of prophecies concerning the end of the world, the return of the dead and the creation of a new earth; there have even been references to "the rain of stars." This is followed by a call to peace and lastly by a dance designed to hasten these events and protect the faithful, in this case the Indians. In a word, these messages from beyond the grave contain eschatological and "millenarian" conceptions such as are to be met with in one form or another in all mythologies and religions.[18]

---

16. Except perhaps among some very degenerate Melanesian tribes.

17. Such practices have become rare, so the writer was told, owing to the fact that their evil consequences too often turned against the guilty, thanks to the protection enjoyed by their intended victims.

18. Certain altogether analogous movements occurred successively in Peru and in Bolivia, from the time of the Spanish conquest to the beginning of the present century.

PLATE IV

The features of the Ghost Dance story which made it so special and so tragic arose out of the physical and psychological conditions prevailing at that moment. The despair of the Indians transposed these prophecies into the immediate future and conferred on them in addition a combative tone quite out of keeping with the pacific character of the original message; nonetheless, it was not the Indians who provoked the conflict. As for the quasi-miraculous experiences of certain believers, especially among the Sioux, they seem to have been not so much phenomena of suggestion as hallucinations due to a collective psychosis and also in part to have been determined by Christian influences. Wovoka always denied having claimed to be the Christ, whereas he never denied having encountered the divine Being—which can be understood in many different ways—nor having received a message; there was, however, no reason why he should deny one thing rather than the other.[19] There seems to be no occasion to accuse Wovoka of imposture, especially as he has been described as a man of sincerity by white men who at least had no prejudice in his favor; doubtless the truth is that he too was a victim of circumstances. To see this whole movement in its proper proportions one must look at it in its traditional context, as determined by the "polyprophetism" of the Indians as well as by the apocalyptic trend common to all religions, and at the same time in its contingent and temporal context, namely, the collapse of the vital foundations of the Plains Indian civilization.

A fascinating combination of combative and stoical heroism with a priestly bearing conferred on the Indian of the Plains and Forests a sort

19. Cf. *The Ghost-Dance Religion* by James Mooney, in the *Fourteenth Annual Report of the Bureau of Ethnology to the Secretary of the Smithsonian Institution*, Washington, 1896; and also *The Prophet Dance of the North-West* by Leslie Spear in *General Series in Anthropology*, Menasha, Wisconsin, 1935.

of majesty at once aquiline and solar; hence the powerfully original and irreplaceable beauty that is associated with the red man and contributes to his prestige as a warrior and as a martyr.[20] Like the Japanese of the time of the Samurai, the Red Indian was in the deepest sense an artist in the outward manifestation of his personality: apart from the fact that his life was a ceaseless sporting with suffering and death,[21] hence also a kind of chivalrous *karma yoga*,[22] the Indian knew how to impart to this spiritual style an aesthetic adornment unsurpassable in its expressiveness.

One factor which may have caused people to regard the Red Indian as an individualist—in principle and not merely de facto—is the crucial importance he attaches to moral worth in men—to "character" if you will—and hence his cult of action.[23] The heroic and silent act is contrasted with the empty and prolix talking of the coward; the Indian's love of secrecy, his reluctance to express what is sacred by means of facile speeches that weaken and disperse it, can be explained in this way. The whole Red Indian character may be summed up in two words, if such a condensation be allowable: the act and the secret; the act shattering if need be, and the secret impassive. Rock-like, the

---

20. With all due deference to the anti-romantic pseudo-realists who believe in nothing but the trivial. If no so-called primitive people has aroused an interest so lively and so lasting as have the Red Indians, and if they incarnate some of our nostalgias often wrongly qualified as puerile, it really must be that they are something in themselves, for "there is no smoke without fire."

21. A "trial by ordeal," as Hartley Burr Alexander described it.

22. Black Elk's son told the writer that among the Indian warriors there were some who vowed to die on the battlefield; they were called "those who do not return," and they carried special insignia, notably a staff adorned with feathers and with a recurved point. Similar information was given by the Crow Indians.

23. "What can never be taken from a man," one Sioux told the writer, "is his upbringing, it can neither be taken away nor sold. Each man must discipline his own character and shape his personality; if he lets himself go, he will fall and he will bear the responsibility for it." No less typical is the following thought as expressed by the same informant: "When an Indian smokes the Pipe, he directs it towards the four directions and towards Heaven and Earth, and after that he must watch his tongue, his actions and his character."

Indian of former times reposed in his own being, his own personality, ready to translate it into action with the impetuosity of lightning; but at the same time he remained humble before the Great Mystery, whose message, he knew, could always be discerned in the Nature around him.

Virgin Nature is at one with holy poverty and also with spiritual childlikeness; she is an open book containing an inexhaustible teaching of truth and beauty. It is in the midst of his own artifices that man most easily becomes corrupted, it is they that make him covetous and impious; close to virgin Nature, who knows neither agitation nor falsehood, he has the hope of remaining contemplative like Nature herself. And it is Nature—quasi-divine in her totality—who, beyond all the erring ways of human beings, will have the final word.

In order fully to understand the abruptness of the breakup of the Red Indian race one must take account of the fact that this race had lived for thousands of years in a kind of paradise that was practically speaking without limits; the Indians of the West were still living under such conditions at the beginning of the nineteenth century. Theirs was a rugged paradise, to be sure, but one that nevertheless provided an environment full of grandeur and of a sacred character, comparable in many respects with the northern parts of Europe before the coming of the Romans.[24] The Indians identified themselves spiritually and humanly with this inviolate Nature—inviolable in their view—and accordingly they accepted all her laws, including the struggle for life, as exemplifying "the principle of the best." But as time went on, and

---

24. The Germans lived in hamlets and the Gauls in towns, but all their buildings were of wood, and this fact marks a fundamental difference between them and the Mediterranean people who lived in stone-built cities.

concordantly with the development of the "Iron Age" in which passions predominate and wisdom disappears, abuses began to arise with increasing frequency; a heroic, but vindictive and cruel, individualism obscured the disinterested virtues, as indeed happened with all other warrior peoples. The privileged situation of the Indians, on the fringe of "History" and of its crushing urban civilizations, had inevitably to come to an end. There is nothing surprising in the fact that this disintegration of a paradise, which had in a certain sense grown old, coincided with modern times.[25]

Nevertheless it is abundantly clear that this account of the situation in terms of its fatality alone is one-sided and cannot extenuate or excuse the villainies of which the Indian has been a victim during several centuries. If that is not so, the concept of justice and injustice is meaningless and there have never been such things as infamy or tragedy. Apologists for the White invasion and its consequences are only too ready to argue that all peoples in all ages have committed acts of violence; violence, yes—but not necessarily acts of baseness, perpetrated, what is more, in the name of liberty, equality, fraternity, civilization, progress and "the rights of man"! The conscious, calculated, methodical, official—and by no means anonymous—destruction of the Red race, its traditions and culture, in North America and partially also in South America, far from having been an unavoidable process—and as such possibly excusable in the name of natural laws, provided one does not oneself claim to have outgrown those laws thanks to "civilization"—this destruction, it must be said, certainly remains one of the greatest crimes and most blatant cases of vandalism in all human history.

---

25. Last Bull, formerly custodian of the sacred arrows of the Cheyennes, told the writer about an ancient prophecy of his tribe according to which a man would come from the East holding a leaf or skin covered with graphic signs; he would show this leaf and declare that it had come from the Creator of the world; and he would destroy men, trees and grasses in order to replace them with other men, other trees, other grasses.

That said, there remains the ineluctable aspect of things, the aspect of fatality, in virtue of which that which is possible cannot but be manifested in one way or another; and all that happens has its causes, be they immediate or remote. However, this aspect of the world and of destiny does not prevent things from being what they are; at its own level, evil remains evil. The nature of evil, and not its inevitability, constitutes its condemnation; its inevitability must be accepted, for tragedy enters perforce into the divine play, if only because the world is not God; one must not accept error, yet one must be resigned to its existence. But beyond earthly destructions there is the Indestructible: "Every form you see," says Rumi, "has its archetype in the divine world, beyond space; if the form perishes what matter, since its heavenly model is indestructible? Every beautiful form you have seen, every meaningful word you have heard—be not sorrowful because all this must vanish, for it is not really thus. The divine Spring is immortal and its flow gives water without cease; since neither the one nor the other can be stopped, wherefore do you lament? . . . From the first moment when you entered this world of existence, a ladder was placed before you. . . ."

The Sacred Pipe

The Indians of North America[1] possess, in their tradition, a symbol and "means of grace" of the first importance: the Sacred Pipe, which represents not only a doctrinal synthesis, both concise and complex, but also a ritual instrument around which centers their whole spiritual and social life. To describe the symbolism of the Sacred Pipe and of its rite is thus, in a certain sense, to expound the sum of Indian wisdom. It will not be necessary to treat this subject here in all its fullness; to do so would be difficult inasmuch as the Red Indian tradition varies consider-

---

Translator's note: This article—with minor variations—appeared as the Introduction to the French translation of *The Sacred Pipe* (op. cit.), *Les Rites Secrets des Indiens Sioux*, Paris, Payot, 1953 and 1975.

1. Or rather, to be more precise: the Indians of the plains and forests which stretch from the Rocky Mountains (and even from farther West) to the Atlantic Ocean.

ably in its forms of expression (as may be seen for example in the myth of the origin of the Calumet and in the symbolism of colors), such variations being due to the scattering of the tribes in the course of the centuries;[2] we will therefore dwell rather upon the fundamental aspects of this wisdom which, as such, remain always the same beneath the variety of the ways in which they are expressed. We will use, however, in preference to others, the doctrinal symbols found among the Sioux, the nation which can be considered, in certain respects, as "central" among Indian peoples, and to which belonged Hehaka Sapa—Black Elk—the venerable author of *The Sacred Pipe*.[3] The teachings of this sage have been particularly precious to us, as much from the point of view of doctrine as from that of living spirituality in our times.

While the Indians of North America are one of the races which have been most studied by ethnographers, it cannot be said that everything about them is fully known, for the simple reason that ethnography does not embrace all possible forms of knowledge—any more than do other ordinary sciences—and therefore cannot possibly be regarded as a general key. There is in fact a sphere which by definition is beyond the reach of ordinary science ("outward" or "profane" science, that is to say), but which is the very basis of every civilization: this is spirituality—the knowledge of Divine Reality and of the means of realizing It, in some degree or other, in oneself. Clearly no one can understand any one form of spirituality without knowing spirituality in itself;[4] to be able to know the wisdom of a people we must first of all

---

2. The same thing is true of Hinduism and perhaps of every tradition which has a mythological form; in Hinduism the same symbols may vary considerably from region to region: the same term may signify a fundamental reality in one place and a secondary aspect of the same reality elsewhere.

3. *The Sacred Pipe*, op. cit. Black Elk died in 1950 on Pine Ridge Reservation (South Dakota).

4. It is quite evident that a knowledge of skull shapes, idioms and folklore customs in no wise qualifies a person for an intellectual penetration of ideas and symbols. Certain ethnologists believe themselves justified in calling "vague" every conception they themselves fail to understand.

possess the keys to such wisdom, and these indispensable keys are to be found, not in any subsidiary branch of learning, but in intellectuality at its purest and most universal level. To disallow that which is the very essence of all true wisdom is to bar ourselves in advance from understanding any wisdom at all; in other words, the forms of a known wisdom are the necessary keys to the understanding of any other wisdom as yet unknown.

Some writers feel the need to question whether the idea of God is really present in the Red Indian religion, because they think they see in it a sort of "pantheism" or "immanentism"; but this misunderstanding is simply due to the fact that most of the Indian terms for the Divinity refer to all Its possible aspects, and not merely, as is the case with the word "God," (at least in practice) to Its personal aspect alone; *Wakan-Tanka* (the "Great Spirit") is God not only as Creator and Lord but also as Impersonal Essence.

Objections are sometimes raised to the name "Great Spirit" as a translation of the Sioux word *Wakan-Tanka*, and of similar terms in other Indian languages; but although *Wakan-Tanka* (and the terms which correspond to it) can also be translated by "Great Mystery" or "Great Mysterious Power" (or even "Great Medicine"), and although "Great Spirit" is no doubt not absolutely adequate, it nonetheless serves quite well enough and in any case conveys the meaning in question better than any other term; it is true that the word "spirit" is rather indefinite, but it has for that very reason the advantage of implying no restriction, and this is exactly what the "polysynthetic" term *Wakan* requires. The expression "Great Mystery" which has been suggested by some as a translation of *Wakan-Tanka* (or of the analogous terms, such as *Wakonda* or *Manitu*, in other Indian languages) is no better than "Great Spirit" at expressing the idea in question: besides, what matters is not whether the term corresponds exactly to what we mean by "Spirit," but whether the ideas expressed by the Red Indian term may be translated by "Spirit" or not.

The Sioux make a clear distinction between the essential aspects of *Wakan-Tanka: Tunkashila* (Grandfather) is *Wakan-Tanka* insofar as He is beyond all manifestation, and even beyond all quality or determination whatsoever; *Ate* (Father) on the other hand is God in Act: the Creator, the Nourisher, the Destroyer. Analogously they make a distinction, as regards the Earth, between *Unchi* (Grandmother) and *Ina* (Mother): *Unchi* is the Substance of all things, whereas *Ina* is her creative act (considered here as "childbearing"), which conjointly with "inspiration" by *Ate*, produces all beings.

It is through the animal species and the phenomena of Nature that the Indian contemplates the angelic Essences and the Divine Qualities; in this connection we will quote from one of Joseph Epes Brown's letters: "It is often difficult for those who look on the tradition of the red man from the outside or through the 'educated' mind, to understand their preoccupation with the animals, and with all things in the Universe. But for these people, as of course for all traditional peoples, every created object is important simply because they know the metaphysical correspondence between this world and the 'Real World.' No object is for them what it appears to be, but it is simply the pale shadow of a Reality. It is for this reason that every created object is *wakan*, holy, and has a power according to the loftiness of the spiritual reality that it reflects; thus many objects possess negative powers as well as those which are positive and good, and every object is treated with respect, for the particular 'power' that it possesses can be transferred into man—of course they know that everything in the Universe has its counterpart in the soul of man. The Indian humbles himself before the whole of creation, especially when 'lamenting' (that is, when he ritually invokes the 'Great Spirit' in solitude), because all visible things were created before him and, being older than he, deserve respect (this priority of created things may also be taken as a symbol of the Priority of the Principle); but although the last of created things, man is also the first, since he alone may know the Great Spirit *(Wakan-Tanka)*."[5]

_____

5. "The Indian's religion is generally spoken of as Nature and Animal worship. The term seems too broadcast and indiscriminate. Careful inquiry and observation fail

This will help to explain in what way every "typical" thing, that is, everything that manifests an "essence," is *wakan*, sacred. To believe that God is the sun is certainly an altogether "pagan" error (and one that is quite foreign to Red Indian thought), but it is just as absurd (at least, metaphysically) to believe that the sun is simply and solely an incandescent mass or, in other words, that in no way whatsoever is it God. We might express the idea like this: *wakan* is whatever conforms integrally to its proper "genius"; the Principle is *Wakan-Tanka*, namely: what is absolutely "Self"; on the other hand a sage is he who is wholly in conformity with his "genius" or with his "essence," with that which is none other than the "Great Spirit" or the "Great Mystery." *Wakan* is what enables us to apprehend directly the Divine Reality; a man is *wakan* when his soul manifests the Divine with the spontaneous and flashing evidence of the wonders of Nature: the elements, the sun, lightning, the eagle. . . . That is why cowardice (a kind of forsaking

---

to show that the Indian actually worships the objects which are set up or mentioned by him in his ceremonies. The earth, the four winds, the sun, moon and stars, the stones, the water, the various animals, are all exponents of a mysterious life and power. . . ." (Alice C. Fletcher, *The Elk Mystery or Festival.*)— "A thing is not only what it is visibly, but also what it represents. Natural or artificial objects are not for the primitive, as they can be for us, arbitrary 'symbols' of some other and higher reality, but actual manifestations of this reality: the eagle or the lion, for example, is not so much a symbol or image *of* the Sun as it *is* the Sun in a likeness (the form being more important than the nature in which it may be manifested); and in the same way every house *is* the world in a likeness, and every altar *is* situated at the centre of the earth; it is only because 'we' are more interested in what things are than in what they mean, more interested in particular facts than in universal ideas, that this is 'inconceivable' to us. Descent from a totem animal is not, then, what it appears to the anthropologist, a literal absurdity, but a descent from the Sun, the Progenitor and *Prajapati* of all, in that form in which he revealed himself whether in vision or in dream, to the founder of the clan. . . . So that, as Lévy-Bruhl says of such symbols, 'very often it is not their purpose to "represent" their prototype to the eye, but to facilitate a participation,' and that 'if it is their essential function to "represent," in the full sense of the word, invisible beings or objects, and to make their presence effective, it follows that they are not necessarily reproductions or likenesses of these beings or objects.'" (Ananda K. Coomaraswamy, *Figures of Speech or Figures of Thought*, London, Luzac & Co., 1946.)

PLATE V

one's "personality") is the foremost sin; and that also explains the Indian "individualism," either seeming or real.

As to the knowledge of the "Great Spirit" which man alone of all earthly creation may attain to, Black Elk once defined it as follows: "I am blind and do not see the things of this world; but when the Light comes from Above, it enlightens my heart and I can see, for the Eye of my heart (Chante Ista) sees everything. The heart is a sanctuary at the center of which there is a little space, wherein the Great Spirit dwells, and this is the Eye (Ista). This is the Eye of the Great Spirit by which He sees all things and through which we see Him. If the heart is not pure, the Great Spirit cannot be seen, and if you should die in this ignorance, your soul cannot return immediately to the Great Spirit, but it must be purified by wandering about in the world. In order to know the center of the heart where the Great Spirit dwells you must be pure and good, and live in the manner that the Great Spirit has taught us. The man who is thus pure contains the Universe in the pocket of his heart (Chante Ognaka)."[6]

All we have said so far may be taken as an illustration of the red race's polysynthetic genius, which makes itself evident most directly in these peoples' languages: just as the verb embraces in itself all the different elements that go to make up the sentence, so the fundamental conception of the "Great Spirit" embraces all the different elements that go to make up thought, which means that the Universe is considered only as it relates to God, and this easily explains why the Indians are suspected of pantheism—always most undiscerningly—by people who have received a philosophical, rationalistic and conceptualistic education. Nothing illustrates better the polysynthetic perspective than

6. As is often the case, the deep-rooted agreement of the traditional doctrines shows itself here even in forms and details. We might recall also the "Eye of the Heart" in the Plotinian doctrine as also in the Augustinian doctrine; no less remarkable is the close parallelism with the description of Brahma-pura as given in the Chhāndogya Upanishad, for instance.

the verses of the *Rigveda* (X.90) in which the world is likened to a part of Universal Man, *Purusha,* the victim of the Primordial Sacrifice whence all beings originate: "This world is nought but *Purusha.* . . . Three quarters of him rose aloft, one quarter of him spread in this world so as to pervade all beings, the animate and the inanimate."

The Sacred Pipe is as it were the central expression of this poly-synthesis: it is the synthesis of all knowledge—the "content" of all knowledge being *Wakan-Tanka,* Who alone "is."

The Calumet was "revealed," or "sent down from Heaven"; its coming into this world is supernatural, as the sacred accounts bear witness.

Before giving a summary account of the symbolism of the Calumet, we cannot do better than quote the explanation which was given of it by Black Elk in the first book whereby he became known to the outside world:[7] "I fill this sacred Pipe with the bark of the red willow; but before we smoke it, you must see how it is made and what it means. These four ribbons hanging here on the stem are the four quarters of the universe. The black one is for the west where the thunder beings live to send us rain; the white one for the north, whence comes the great white cleansing wind: the red one for the east, whence springs the light and where the morning star lives to give men wisdom; the yellow for the south, whence come the summer and the power to grow. But these four spirits are only one Spirit after all, and this eagle feather here is for that One, which is like a father, and also it is for the thoughts of men that should rise high as eagles do. Is not the sky a father and the earth a mother, and are not all living things with feet or wings or roots their children? And this hide upon the mouthpiece

---

7. *Black Elk Speaks,* op. cit.

here, which should be bison hide, is for the earth, from whence we came and at whose breast we suck as babies all our lives, along with all the animals and birds and trees and grasses. And because it means all this, and more than any man can understand, the Pipe is holy."

When the Indian performs the rite of the Calumet, he greets the sky, the earth and the four cardinal points, either by offering them the Pipe, stem forward (in accordance with the ritual of the Sioux, for example), or by blowing the smoke towards the different directions, and sometimes also towards the "central fire"[8] burning in front of him; the order of these gestures may vary, but their static plan remains always the same, since it is the doctrinal figure of which the rite is to be the enactment.

In keeping with certain ritual practices, we will begin our enumeration with the West: the West Wind brings with it, as we have already seen, thunder and rain, that is, Revelation and also Grace; the North Wind purifies and gives strength; from the East comes Light, that is, Knowledge, and these, according to the Indian perspective, go together with Peace; the South is the source of Life and Growth; it is there that the "Good Red Road" begins, the way of welfare and felicity. The Universe thus depends on four primordial determinations—Water, Cold, Light, Warmth; the first of these, Water, is none other than the positive aspect of darkness which should normally stand in opposition to light, just as cold is the opposite of warmth; the positive aspect of darkness is in fact its quality of shade which gives protection against

---

8. "The fire of his council or of his great medicine lodge, as some of his songs bear witness, is the oldest of all: it is practically the same as what the Greek philosophers of the school of Pythagoras named Hestia, which burns at the centre of the earth. It is in this central fire that he takes part by mingling his breath with the fire of the sacred tobacco, and it is the same fire which rises with its smoke towards the zenith of the universe or sinks to the nadir, touching the earth, or joins the four winds which, filled with the beautiful life of the high heavens, blow round about our human habitation." (Hartly Burr Alexander, *The Art and Philosophy of the North American Indians*, Paris, E. Leroux, 1926.)

the parching strength of the sun and which produces or favors moisture; the sky must grow dark before it can give rain, and God manifests Anger (thunder) before granting Grace, of which rain is the natural symbol. As to Cold ("the sanctifying and purifying wind which gives strength"), its positive aspect is purity so that the Purity of the North may be placed in opposition to the Warmth of the South, just as the Rain of the West is opposable to the Light from the East; the connection between Cold and Purity is evident: inanimate, cold things, that is, minerals—unlike animate, warm beings—are not subject to corruption. The Light of the East is, as we have already said, Knowledge; and Warmth is Life and therefore Love, and also Goodness, Beauty, Happiness.

Before going further, we may reply to an objection which might arise from the fact that in the Sioux mythology, the Four Winds seem to correspond to a rather secondary function of the Divinity, which is here divided into four Aspects, each of which contains four subdivisions. The Sioux doctrine, by a remarkable derogation of the ordinary mythological hierarchy, gives a preeminence to these four Principles over the other Divinities, showing thereby very clearly that, in the rite of the Calumet or rather in the perspective that goes with it, the cardinal points represent the four essential Divine Manifestations.

It should moreover never be forgotten that among other Indians this symbolism takes on forms very different from those to be found among the Sioux: thus (to cite a single example) the four Principles are symbolized among the Arapaho by four Old Men sprung from the Sun who watch over the inhabitants of the terrestrial world and to whom are attributed symbolically the day (South-East), summer (South-West), night (North-West) and winter (North-East). Finally, it is worth noting that the Quaternary is often considered in the last analysis as constituting a Duodecad, each element being considered under three aspects, quite apart from the vertical axis of Heaven and Earth which adds two new elements to the Quaternary, though these are not of the same order. We cannot dwell on all of these variations, and we need only stress the fact that they are independent of the Quaternary Principle which alone concerns us here.

Coming back now to the consideration of the four Principles: it would also be possible to speak of the four "cosmic Places" in the following terms, here again, as always, starting from the West and moving towards the North: Moisture, Cold, Drought, Warmth; the West's negative aspect, the correlative of moisture, is darkness, and the East's positive aspect, the correlative of drought, is light. The Thunderbird (*Wakinyan-Tanka*) whose abode is in the West, and who protects the earth and its vegetation against drought and death, is said to flash lightning from its eyes and to thunder with its wings;[9] the analogy with the Revelation on Mount Sinai, which was accompanied by "thunders and lightnings, and a thick cloud" (Exod. 19:16) is all the more striking in that this Revelation took place on a rock, while in the Indian mythology it is precisely the Rock which is connected with the Thunderbird, as we shall see from what follows. As to the symbolic connection between Revelation and the West, it may seem unusual and even paradoxical, but it should always be remembered that in Indian symbolism the cardinal points are necessarily positive in their meaning: thus, as we have already said, the West is not the opposite of the East, not Darkness and ignorance, but the positive complement of the East, that is rain and Grace. It might also seem surprising that the Indian

---

9. According to Iroquois mythology, "Hino, the Spirit of Thunder . . . is the guardian of Heaven. Armed with a powerful bow and arrows of fire (flashes of lightning), he destroys áll harmful things. His consort 'The Rainbow' . . . Oshadagea, 'The Great Eagle of the Dew,' is also at the service of Hino. He lives in the Heaven of the West and carries in the hollow of his back a lake of dew. When the maleficent fire sprites destroy all the earth's greenery, Oshadagea takes flight and from his outspread wings the beneficent moisture flows drop by drop." (Max Fauconnet: *Mythologies des deux Amériques*, in *Mythologie Générale* of the *Librairie Larousse*).— This association of the lightning with the Thunderbird is all the more remarkable in that the most diverse traditions connect lightning with Revelation, just as they connect rain with Grace. The eagle and the lightning belong to the same universal symbolism; hence in the Christian tradition the association of the eagle with Saint John, Revealer of the Apocalypse and "Son of Thunder."

tradition should establish a symbolical link between the West Wind, bearer of thunder and rain, and the Rock which is an angelic or semidivine personification of a cosmic Aspect of *Wakan-Tanka*; but this connection is admissible, for in the rock are united the same complementary aspects as in the thunderstorm: the terrible aspect by reason of its destructive hardness (the rock is, for the Indians, a symbol of destruction—hence his stone weapons of which the connection with thunderbolts is obvious), and the aspect of Grace through its giving birth to springs which, like the rain, quench the thirst of the land.[10]

There still remains something to be said about the association of the Winds with the cardinal points: these four Winds are the Productive Forces (in the sense of the Sanskrit word *Shakti*) of the Quarters of the World, and they are conceived of as encircling the whole horizon and deciding the issues of life on earth by their combined influences. The wind is as the "breath" of this earthly world in which we live, so that it represents the "breathing" of the cosmos. The breath is in a certain sense the vehicle of the "soul" or the "spirit," whence the etymological connection between these words in many languages; but it is also the active vehicle of life, for it nourishes and purifies the blood,

---

10. It should be mentioned here that in the world of the Red Indian the "rocks," namely the Rocky Mountains, lie to the West and give birth to a number of rivers by which the plains are fertilized; this is an example, among many others, of sacred geography.—"When a vision comes from the thunder beings of the West, it comes with terror like a thunderstorm; but when the storm of vision has passed, the world is greener and happier; for whenever the truth of vision comes upon the world, it is like a rain. The world, you see, is happier after the terror of the storm." (*Black Elk Speaks*, op. cit.)— Asceticism springs from the same cosmic connection between terror and Grace, and here again the Indian tradition does not differ from other forms of spirituality: "'To make medicine' is to engage upon a special period of fasting, thanksgiving, prayer and self-denial, even of self-torture . . . The procedure is entirely a devotional exercise. The purpose is to subdue the passions of the flesh and to improve the spiritual self. The bodily abstinence and the mental concentration upon lofty thoughts cleanses both the body and the soul . . . Then the individual mind gets closer towards conformity with the mind of the Great Medicine above us." (Wooden Leg—a Cheyenne Indian—in his book: *A Warrior who Fought Custer*, Lincoln, University of Nebraska Press, 1962.)

PLATE VI

life's passive, lower vehicle. The breath then, is thus both "soul" and "life" and thus it is made in the image of the Divine Word whose creative Breath made man himself.

As we have already mentioned, the cardinal points are associated symbolically with four Divinities which are referred to in many different ways, and which personify four complementary aspects of the universal Spirit; the Spirit unites these aspects in Itself as colors are unified in the light; and this fourfold Spirit "is" *Wakan-Tanka* in the sense that it enjoys identity with God in virtue of the Oneness of Essence, just as the light enjoys essential identity with the sun. According to the cosmology of the Sioux, each of these Divinities (or rather Semi-Divinities) is subdivided in its turn into four entities which rank one above the other in hierarchy and which are called by the most diverse names, such as Sun, Moon, Bison, Soul, each entity being an offshoot or reflection of the Spirit in the cosmos; these ramifications are in fact the secondary Angels whose numberless modalities penetrate as far as the confines of creation. The four Divine Powers may also clearly be conceived of as beyond manifestation, in the purely Principial Reality of *Wakan-Tanka;* they will then represent His fourfold Polarization, His Unity or Transcendence being always represented in the rite of the Calumet by the Sky; or in other terms, the highest Angels are the reflections, in creation, of the essential Divine Qualities, so that the names of these Angels may be applied to these uncreated Qualities, and inversely.

In general, by reason of his polysynthetic or "vertical" perspective (we might say his "primordial" perspective) the Indian will tend to take a simultaneous view of the different hierarchized aspects of one and the same reality: he will tend to look on them as unified by their co-essentiality, so that, for example, the Earth will not be for him simply perceptible matter or simply the universal Substance, but both at the same time, the one in the other; the matter that his senses perceive will be for him the material appearance of the Divine Substance, thus the Divine Substance in its manifestation of materiality. This point of view shows itself in the very symbolism of the Thunderbird who is *Wakan-Tanka* as seen under the particular aspect of Revelation: like the thunderbolt, with which it is symbolically associated, the eagle pierces space, from Sky (of which it is the incarnation) to Earth; in other words, the Thunderbird forms a link, by its presence, between Heaven and all the lower degrees of "cosmic space."

But let us revert to the symbolism of the Four Winds: the Sioux draw an analogy between these and the four periods of the cycle, which are symbolized by the four eagle feathers that adorn the sacred hoop used in the Sun Dance and on other occasions: the first period is that of the Stone, the second that of the Bow, the third that of the Fire, and the fourth that of the Pipe, each of these symbols representing the spiritual means characteristic of the respective period. There are like-wise four ages through which every created thing must pass: the first is the South which is yellow and represents the source of all life, and this is the first age in a historical cycle; the second is the West, which is black; the third the North, which is white; and the fourth the East, which is red; earthly humanity is now in the fourth age which will end with a great disaster. This scheme of things which attributes the "Gol-den Age" to the North and the "Iron Age" to the West may seem at first surprising, but two things must here be taken into consideration: firstly, as regards the Golden Age, if it be correct to attribute it to the North—the earthly Paradise being, according to tradition, situated in the polar region—it is nonetheless true that in actual fact the North Pole is now covered with ice, and that in a qualitative sense the South[11] does really correspond to Paradise and thus to the Golden Age,

---

11. This applies to the Northern hemisphere.

so that the symbolism in question may be based on the warmth and fertility of the South just as well as on the Hyperborean situation of the Primordial Garden; secondly, as regards the Iron Age, if it be obviously correct to attribute it, according to the geographical perspective of the Old World, to the West, since it is there that the sun sets and there also that has arisen that final subversion which is spreading its shadows over the whole of humanity, it is nonetheless true that for the Indians this same subversion comes from the East; it is there that they situate what for the Orientals is the "dark West," and thence have come those "palefaced spirits" by whom the red race has been practically exterminated; but this does not prevent them from expecting that the universal Savior, the Messiah awaited by all peoples at the end of the Iron Age, will also come from the East, so that the solar symbolism of this direction remains intact in the Sioux theory of the four cyclic periods. Moreover, according to the cosmology of the Cheyenne Indians, the Primordial Tradition originally was established in the Arctic: the earthly Paradise lay in the far North on an island risen from the primordial waters; there, Spring was perpetual and men and animals spoke the same language. Then came tribulations (for example, two floods) after which the red race, or rather its primordial ancestors, settled definitively in the South which in its turn had become a fertile region.

We must not forget to mention here that the Calumet has, besides its fourfold symbolism, a threefold one which relates to the three worlds and to which correspond respectively the sky, the cardinal points and the earth. The three worlds are also represented, among the Crow Indians, in the form of three rings painted on the central pole of the Sun Dance, this pole signifying the Tree of Life or the World Axis, in accordance with the Hyperborean symbolism;[12] they are then inter-

12. "It should be remembered . . . that in diverse traditions the image of the Sun is also connected with the image of the tree, . . . being represented as the fruit of the 'World Tree'; it leaves its tree at the beginning of the cycle and comes back to rest there at the end so that . . . the tree is in fact 'the Station of the Sun.'" (René Guénon, "L'Arbre du Monde," in *Etudes Traditionnelles,* February, 1939).

preted as making up the triad (in ascending order) body, soul, Spirit or gross, subtle, Pure.

We now come to another aspect of the rite of the Calumet, and here may be seen the analogy between the smoke of the sacred tobacco (*kinnikinnik*) and incense: in most religions incense is as it were a human response to the Divine Presence[13] and the smoke marks the spiritual presence of man in the encounter with the supernatural[14] Presence of God, as is affirmed by this Iroquois incantation: "Hail! Hail! Hail! Thou Who has created all things, hear our voice. We are obeying Thy Commandments. That which Thou hast created returneth back unto Thee. The smoke of the holy plant riseth up unto Thee, whereby it may be seen that our speech is true."[15]

In the rite of the Calumet man represents the state of individuation; space (with its six directions) represents the Universal into which what is individual has—after being transmuted—to be reabsorbed; the smoke disappearing into space, with which it finally identifies itself,

---

13. This Presence is symbolized among the Indians by the eagle feather; the eagle represents the Great Spirit.

14. This adjective is not a pleonasm, for the "natural" Presence of God is none other than Existence and its diverse expressions and forms, such as the symbols of Nature—Sun, Moon, Bison and others—which for the Indian are all *wakan,* sacred.— We will quote here the following deeply symbolic explanation which was given by an Indian chief to the well known ethnologist Alice C. Fletcher: "Everything as it moves, now and then, here and there, makes stops. The bird as it flies stops in one place to make its nest, and in another to rest in its flight. A man when he goes forth stops when he wills. So God has stopped. The sun, which is so bright and beautiful, is one place where He has stopped. The moon, the stars, the winds He has been with. The trees, the animals, are all where He has stopped, and the Indian thinks of these places and sends his prayers there to reach the place where God has stopped and win help and a blessing."

15. Quoted by Paul Radin in his *Histoire de la Civilisation Indienne,* Paris, Payot, 1953.

exemplifies well this transmutation from the hard, opaque or formal into the dissolved, transparent or formless; it exemplifies at the same time the unreality of the ego and so of the world which, spiritually, is identical with the human microcosm. But this resorption of the smoke into space (which stands for God) transcribes at the same time the Mystery of "Identity" in virtue of which, to use a Sufic expression, "the Sage is not created"; it is only in illusion that man is a volume cut out of space and isolated in it: in reality he "is" that space and he must "become what he is," as the Hindu Scriptures say.[16] By absorbing, together with the sacred smoke, the perfume of Grace, and by breathing himself out with it towards the unlimited, man spreads himself supernaturally throughout the Divine Space, so to speak: but at the same time God is represented by the fire which consumes the tobacco. The tobacco itself represents man or, from the macrocosmic point of view, the Universe; space is here incarnate in the fire of the Calumet, just as, according to another symbolism, the cardinal points are united in the Central Fire.

According to Black Elk, "Everything an Indian does is done in a circle, and that is because the Power of the World always works in circles and everything tries to be round. In the old days when we were a

16. The symbolism of the Tibetan Buddhist "prayer wheel" is inversely analogous to that of the Calumet: whereas in relation to the Calumet, the Divine Reality is to be found in the directions of space towards which tend (starting from the center, which is the state of individuation) the spiritual aspirations of the individual, the "prayer wheel" represents the Divine Reality in the form of a revealed Utterance or *mantra* which is fixed in space by the sacred letters that transcribe it and which through its rotation blesses the Universe as manifested in space. According to an Upanishad: *"Brahma* is to the north, to the south, to the east, to the west, at the zenith and at the nadir."— In the same way the Koran says: "Wheresoever ye turn, there is the face of *Allāh."*

strong and happy people, all our power came to us from the sacred
hoop of the nation, and so long as the hoop was unbroken, the people
flourished. The flowering tree was the living center of the hoop, and
the circle of the four quarters nourished it. The East gave peace and
light, the South gave warmth, the West gave rain, and the North with
its cold and mighty wind gave strength and endurance. This knowledge came to us from the outer [transcendent or universal] World
together with our religion. Everything the Power of the World does is
done in a circle. The sky is round, and I have heard that the earth is
round like a ball, and so are all the stars. The wind, in its greatest
power, whirls. Birds make their nests in circles, for theirs is the same
religion as ours . . . Our tepees were round like the nests of birds, and
these were always set in a circle, the nation's hoop, a nest of many
nests, where the Great Spirit meant us to hatch our children."[17]

All the static forms of existence, whether they be material or mental, are thus as it were determined by a concentric archetype: centered
in his qualitative, "totemic," almost impersonal ego, the Indian tends
towards independence and so towards indifference with regard to the
outward world; he surrounds himself with silence as with a magic circle, and this silence is sacred as being the vehicle of the heavenly influences. It is from this silence—of which the natural support is solitude—
that the Indian draws his spiritual strength; his ordinary prayer is
unvoiced: what it requires is not thought but consciousness of the
Spirit, and this consciousness is immediate and formless like the vault
of heaven. [18]

If the Great Spirit works always "in circles," He works also, in
another respect, always "in fours," as may be seen from the directions
of space and the cycles of time (and then the circle turns into the swas-

---

17. *Black Elk Speaks*, op. cit.

18. Needless to say, such an attitude of worship presupposes a mental heredity
which no mere individual initiative could possibly replace.

PLATE VII

tika, which is an important Red Indian symbol): that is why the Indian, whose course of life lies as it were between the central point and limitless space, makes static things according to the circular or unitive principle, and dynamic things (actions) according to the quaternary principle,[19] that is, in conformity with the four cardinal virtues which are for him: courage, patience, generosity and fidelity. This profound structure of Indian life signifies that the red man has no intention of fixing himself on this earth where everything, according to the law of stabilization and also of condensation (petrification, one might say) is liable to crystallize; and this explains the Indian's aversion for houses, especially stone ones, and also the absence of a writing which, from this perspective, would fix and kill the sacred flow of the Spirit. The European civilization, on the other hand, in both its dynamic and static forms, is thoroughly sedentary and urban: it is thus anchored in space where it spreads itself quantitatively, whereas the Indian civilization has its pivot as it were outside space in the unlocalized, principial center; its expansivity is therefore qualitative, in the sense that it is pure movement, symbolizing the limitless, and not a quantitative, not to say mercantile, setting of boundaries to the extension of space. It should be clearly understood in this connection that Christianity, like other religions of the Old World, establishes the Celestial on the earthly plane and builds sanctuaries in the most static of materials, stone; the religion of the Indians, on the other hand, integrates the earthly (the spatial) with the omnipresent Celestial, and that is why the red man's sanctuary is everywhere; that is also why the earth should remain

---

19. The circle has also a dynamic symbolism, in relation to the cross considered in its static symbolism; (we are not referring to the square—the static form par excellence—since it does not enter into this nomadic perspective). If the cross represents, not a centrifugal tendency, but the cardinal points, the circle will represent, not a concentric tendency, but the circular movement of the Four Winds about the world, that is, the passage of the four cosmic Principles from potency to act; the same image is to be found in the swastika, where the plain cross is obviously static and the hooks dynamic and rotatory.

intact, virgin and sacred, as when it left the Divine Hands—since only what is pure reflects the Eternal.[20] The Indian is nothing of a "pantheist," nor does he imagine for one moment that God is in the world; but he knows that the world is mysteriously plunged in God.

What has just been said enables one to understand why Indian art is of an altogether primordial simplicity; its language is concentrated, direct and bold; like the Indian himself (a very noble human type and also one of the most powerfully original), his art is both qualitative and spontaneous; it is precise in its symbolism, while keeping at the same time a surprising freshness. It serves as a "framework" for man, and this explains the high quality of the Indian art of clothing: his majestic headdresses (above all, his great array of eagle feathers), his garments streaming with fringes and embroidered with solar symbols, the bright-patterned moccasins which seem designed to take away from the feet all heaviness and all uniformity, the feminine robes of an exquisite simplicity—this Red Indian art is certainly one of the most vigorous expressions of human genius.

---

20. This perspective explains the great "nomadic revolutions" which, starting from the Mongolian steppes with an unheard of impetuosity, set out to sweep the towns—places of corruption and "petrification"—from the surface of the earth; there is much evidence to show that these conquerors were conscious of carrying out a Divine Decree. In any case, it cannot be denied that the materialistic and quantitative civilization of the modern world represents a peak of urban "incrustation," and that, but for sedentarism, such a civilization could never have come into existence; in fact it crushes nomadism everywhere, or rather, it crushes everything; it will end by crushing even itself. Let us add that the ring of Ghengiz Khan had on it the swastika which, as we have already mentioned, is also often to be found in the symbolic art of the Red Indians. As to the attitude of the Red Indian towards Nature on the one hand and cities on the other, Tacitus describes exactly analogous traits among the ancient Germans: "They think it would be degrading to the majesty of the Gods to imprison them between walls and to represent them by means of a human figure: they consecrate the woods and forests to them, and invoke, by the names of the divinities, that Mystery which they view solely with reverential fear" (. . . *deorumque nominibus appellant Secretum illud, quod sola reverentia vident*). "It is well known that the Germans have no cities and will not even tolerate that their dwellings be touching one another."— Ammonius Marcellus, a fourth century author, reports that the Germans regarded the Roman cities with horror, as being prisons and tombs, and that, after having captured them, they abandoned them.

We have seen that Nature (landscape, sky, stars, elements, wild animals) is a necessary support for the Indian tradition, just as temples are for other religions;[21] all the limitations imposed upon Nature by artificial, ponderous, immovable constructs (limitations that are likewise imposed upon man through his becoming a slave to these constructs) are thus sacrilegious, even "idolatrous," and they carry within themselves the seeds of death. Considered from this point of view the destiny of the red man is tragic in the true sense of the word—a tragedy being a desperate situation caused not by chance but by the fatal clash of two principles. The crushing of the Indian race is tragic because in its deepest and most intimate nature this noble people was opposed to "assimilation"; the red man could only conquer or die; it is the spiritual basis of this alternative which confers on the destiny of the red race an aspect of grandeur and martyrdom.[22] It was not sim-

---

21. As a "Keeper of the Pipe" once said to Joseph Epes Brown, God shows His goodness by leaving Nature intact: "Although we have been crushed by the white man in every possible way, we still have much cause to be thankful to the Great Spirit, for even in this period of darkness His work in Nature remains unchanged and is a continual reminder of the Divine Presence."

22. It is hard to say which was the more ignoble, the treacherous methods employed during the white expansion westwards, or the treatment inflicted on the Indians after their defeat. "The attempts to suppress native leadership and Indian social controls began under the agent who came to Pine Ridge in 1879 . . . Only through the acceptance of stock raising and settlement on farm tracts, he sincerely felt, could the Indian adjust to his new situation. However, like all people of his time, the agent also felt that this must be accompanied by a complete abandonment of Indian custom. Thus, when the Indians seemed to cling too tenaciously to camping by band groups, holding council by themselves, or being uncooperative, he withheld rations or utilized the police to force a change. . . . The undermining of native controls and native leadership was followed later by official regulations which forbade native dances, ceremonies, and pagan customs. . . Children were virtually kidnapped to force them into government schools, their hair was cut, and their Indian clothes thrown away. They were forbidden to speak in their own language . . . those who persisted in clinging to their old ways and those who ran away and were recaptured were thrown into jail. Parents who objected were also jailed. Where possible, children were kept in school year after year to avoid the influence of their families." (Gordon Macgregor, *Warriors without Weapons*, Chicago, University of Chicago Press, 1975.)

ply because they were the weaker side that the Indians succumbed; they did so because they represented a nobility and a spirituality that was incompatible with the white man's commercialism[23]—because they embodied a character, an idea, a principle, and, being what they were, they could not be unfaithful to themselves. This great drama might be defined as the struggle, not only between urban civilization (in the strictly human and pejorative sense of this term, with all its implications of artifice and servility) and the kingdom of Nature considered as the majestic, pure, limitless raiment of the Divine Spirit. And it is from this idea of the final victory of Nature (final because it is primordial) that the Indians draw their inexhaustible patience in the face of the misfortunes of their race; Nature, of which they feel themselves to be embodiments, and which is at the same time their sanctuary, will end by conquering this artificial and sacrilegious world, for it is the Garment, the Breath, the very Hand of the Great Spirit.

---

23. "Cain, who killed his brother, Abel, the herdsman, and built himself a city, prefigures modern civilization, one that has been described from within as a 'murderous machine, with no conscience and no ideals' (G. La Piana), 'neither human nor normal nor Christian' (Eric Gill), and in fact 'an anomaly, not to say a monstrosity' (René Guénon). It has been said: 'The values of life are slowly ebbing. There remains the show of civilization, without any of its realities' (A. N. Whitehead). Criticisms such as these could be cited without end. Modern civilization, by its divorce from any principle, can be likened to a headless corpse of which the last motions are convulsive and insignificant. It is not, however, of suicide, but of murder that we propose to speak." (Ananda K. Coomaraswamy, *Am I My Brother's Keeper?*, Freeport, New York, Books for Libraries Press, 1967.)—"Savages we call them, because their manners differ from ours, which we think the perfection of civility; they think the same of theirs. . . . Having few artificial wants, they have abundance of leisure for improvement by conversation. Our laborious manner of life, compared with theirs, they esteem slavish and base; and the learning, on which we value ourselves, they regard as frivolous and useless." (Benjamin Franklin, *Remarks concerning the Savages of North America*, Dublin, printed for L. White, 1784.)

Symbolism of a Vestimentary Art

When one stands in the midst of a plain, three things strike one's vision: the immense circle of the horizon; the immense vault of the sky; the four cardinal points. It is these elements which primordially determine the spirit and soul of the Indians; it could be said that the whole of their metaphysics or cosmology is based upon these initial motifs. The son of the famous Black Elk explained to the author that the entire religion of the Indians could be represented by a cross inscribed in a circle; the Great Spirit always works in circles, his father had said, and the cross is the well-known doctrine of the four directions of space, upon which is founded the rite of the Calumet. Circle of the Earth, circle of the Sky; East, South, West, North.

The art of the Indians, of the Plains Indians above all—for it is they whom we have in view primarily—makes extensive use of these symbols. We are thinking here a priori of two particularly important motifs: the large sun, whose rays are eagle feathers, and which may be composed of several concentric circles, and the rosette embroidered with porcupine quills which often adorns the clothing, that of the men especially. The designs of these rosettes consist of a combination of circles and radii; thus they are always an image of the sun or the cosmos.

Metaphysically speaking, there are two possible relationships between the relative and the Absolute, or between the world and God—between *māyā* and *Ātmā,* the Hindus would say—and these are on the one hand the relationship of analogy, and on the other that of projection; the first is discontinuous, for nothing in the world could be part of God; the second is continuous, for every symbol is a projection of God. The first relationship is that of transcendence, and the second, that of immanence; all metaphysics, whether Platonic, Vedantic or other, is contained in these two relationships. If the Indians kill buffalo, it is because they know that in this respect the buffalo is not divine, that it is a perishable creature like any other; if on the contrary they reconcile themselves with the buffalo through the rite of the Calumet, thanking it for having furnished them with their subsistence, it is because they know that in this respect the animal is the projection or prolongation of the immortal and quasi-divine archetype. These are the two relationships which the concentric circles and the centrifugal radii represent respectively in the embroidered rosettes as well as in the feathered sun.

The eagle feather, like the eagle itself, represents the Great Spirit in general and the Divine Presence in particular, as certain Sioux explained to us;[1] thus it is plausible that the rays of the sun, itself the image of the Great Spirit, be symbolized by feathers. But these very stylized feathers forming the sun composed of concentric circles also

---

1. We employ the term "Great Spirit" despite all the objections which have been raised against it, and which seem to us to lack sufficient foundation.

symbolize the cocoon, symbol of vital potentiality; now, life and solar radiation coincide for obvious reasons.

One of the most powerful symbols of the sun is the majestic headdress of eagle feathers: whoever wears it is identified with the solar orb, and it is easy to understand that not everyone is qualified to wear it; its splendor—unique of its kind among all traditional headdresses in the world—suggests both royal and priestly dignity, hence the radiance of the hero and the sage. In the past, each feather in the bonnet had to be won; "noblesse oblige," according to a French expression which has become proverbial; one does not identify with the sun without paying a price.

Let us return now to another solar symbol, the medallion—or rosette—decorated with porcupine quills: the quills themselves symbolize the rays of the sun, which gives to the solar design an additional magical quality. The rosette itself represents either the sun or a star, or again the four directions of space or the thunderstorm—depending upon the design used—or some other object or phenomenon; sometimes colors add an additional symbolism to these meanings, connected, it would appear, with cosmic cycles. These rosettes primarily serve to decorate garments: they are then placed either in the middle or on both sides of the chest, or again on the shoulders of certain feminine costumes; they are also placed on the sleeves and on leggings, sometimes on moccasins. In some tribes, they are found on tipis and on all kinds of household objects or implements, on cradleboards, for example, and even on playing balls; but most often they decorate blankets, where they are placed on an embroidered band which runs along the breadth of the blanket, this arrangement being combined at times with the feathered sun. At the center of the rosette there often hang two ribbons embroidered with porcupine quills—or two bunches of horsehair—no doubt two complementary modes of energy, one active and the other passive.

The making of these small masterpieces constitutes a rather complex rite for the women, exactly as is the case for the men when they paint the feathered sun—or some other symbol—on a buffalo hide or on a tipi, or when they decorate their shields with some protective sign.

The introduction of glass beads by white traders gave rise among the Indians to new, more intricate, decorative motifs—still symbolical and strictly geometrical—and to new creations, such as the fully beaded yoke of women's dresses. The floral motifs originated among the woodlands tribes, and were partly influenced by the designs of the whites; they are found especially among the Indians of Canada and the tribes of the North, as far as the Crows. These motifs do not harmonize well with the typical style of the Plains—which accounts for their lack of success—all the more so in that they seem to be more decorative than symbolic.

A very typical element of Indian dress is fringe; first of all, the fringes recall rain, which is a very important image since rain is a message from heaven to earth. But they also symbolize the spiritual fluid of the human person—his *orenda*, as the Iroquois would say, or his *barakah*, as would say the Arabs. This observation is all the more plausible when it is realized that instead of the fringes, Indian shirts are often decorated with horsehair or with scalps; now hair, as is known, is supposed to vehicle a magical power, an *orenda* precisely. We may also say that the fringes are derived from the feathers of a bird, of the eagle above all: arms adorned with fringes are "magically" and spiritually equivalent to the wings of an eagle. There are dances which quite clearly demonstrate this analogy; they evoke the Hindu Garuda, the messenger eagle of the gods, the steed of Vishnu, which once again indicates the relationship between the eagle and the sun.

The existence of princely and priestly garments among the most diverse peoples proves that clothing confers a personality upon man;

PLATE VIII

that it expresses or manifests a function which surpasses the empirical individual. By manifesting a function, the garment represents its corresponding moral and spiritual qualities; to be sure, costume does not change man *ex opere operato*, yet in the normally predisposed individual —hence one who is sensitive to duties and virtues—it actualizes a given awareness of the norm and a given conformity to the archetype.[2] Thus it goes without saying that the costume expresses the mentality of a people; it is absurd to admire as an aesthete or artist the "Indian panache" while denying, with a pseudo-realistic anti-romanticism, the existence of the "noble red man."

It is moreover a curious fact that many people love the Indians, but that hardly anyone dares to admit it; unless they admit it with certain reservations, which all too ostentatiously allow them to disidentify themselves from Rousseau's "good savage" as well as from Cooper's "noble savage"; no one wishes to be taken for a child. Doubtless there is nothing worth retaining in the unrealisitc sentimentalities of a Rousseau, and the least that can be said is that the Indians have no need of them; but as for the "noble savage," this image is not drawn entirely "out of thin air," if only for the simple reason that warlike peoples, by the very fact that they regularly and vocationally court suffering and death and have a cult of self-mastery, possess nobility and grandeur by the nature of things.

The prestige enjoyed by the Indians in the most diverse milieus and countries is explained by the truly fascinating combination of a heroism both stoic and intrepid and the extraordinary expressiveness of their faces, garments and implements, without forgetting—from the

---

2. "If a French proverb says that 'the habit does not make the monk,' there exists a German proverb which says exactly the opposite: *Kleider machen Leute,* 'clothes make the man' . . . Everyone can observe how the quality of a particular garment modifies our behavior: it is because the individual tends to efface himself before the function, so that he is as it were remodeled by the costume." (Jean Hani, *La Divine Liturgie,* Paris, Editions de la Maisnie, 1981, the chapter *"Dramatis Personae."*)

psychological and spiritual point of view—a priestly and contemplative, and so to speak mythological, climate.[3] Some people have maintained that interest in the Red Indians stems from a "false view": it would seem that this interest is explained solely by the nostalgia of urban dwellers and by a desire for escape, whereas in reality—according to this thesis—the Indians in their freedom, condemned to such a hard and dangerous life, were in no wise happy men—no more, so it would seem, than are eagles, free but condemned to struggle for their subsistence. Yet, aside from the fact that the Indians of the past never missed a chance to proclaim that they loved their way of life, we see no relationship between our sympathy for the Indians and a hypothetical desire to hunt buffalo or make war; the friends of the Indians are not all naive men, and there are some who have no desire to spend their life on the prairies. It is true that the hectic and crushing life in the modern world—joined to a total lack of beauty—creates and justifies a desire for escape: it is at least honorable to have more in one's head than professional overwork in airless cities. But if it is merely to justify a nostalgia, we do not see why others besides the Red Indians could not bear the burden, the Zulus or the Dayaks for example. In short, no one can make us believe that if there are intelligent men who admire a Tecumseh, a Black Hawk, a Red Cloud, a Sitting Bull and a Rolling Thunder (Chief Joseph), it is for the sole reason that they feel stifled in their professional life.

Having said this, we have still another remark to make. If it is hypocritical and absurd to call an unmistakable and organized genocide a "historical fatality," it is equally aberrant to accuse "the Americans"—and them alone—of having killed the red man, for there are no "Amer-

---

3. The fact that the Indian of heroic times is perpetuated in children's games almost everywhere in the entire world—and sometimes even in adult games, especially in America and Germany—is not an accident devoid of meaning; it indicates in any case an original and powerful message that cannot die and survives as best it can.

icans"; the white inhabitants of the New World are European immigrants, no more no less, and it is not these immigrants who invented the indiscriminate and lethal "civilizationism," nor the "democratic" prejudice that the opinion of the majority takes precedence over truth. Inasmuch as he embodies virgin Nature, the sense of the sacred and the disdain for money, the Indian was killed in advance in Europe, in men's minds, independently of the conquest of the New World; and if the Indian has had his defenders and friends in Europe, he also had them, and well before, in America itself.

The Demiurge in
North American Mythology

In all the variants of North American mythology, below the Supreme Spirit or Great Mystery there appears a sort of demiurge who is both beneficent and terrible—an initiatory hero and a buffoon, or even a demon. We find the same characteristics also in Hermes, Hercules, Prometheus, Epimetheus and Pandora, and in Nordic mythology, in Loki—half-god and half-giant, and both the enemy and the friend of the other divinities—without forgetting, in the Japanese pantheon, the terrible Susano-o-no-Mikoto, spirit of the tempest and, in a way, the *princeps huius mundi*. There seems to be no mythology from which the jesting or mischievous demigod is wholly absent, but it is perhaps in the mythology of the North American Indians that it has attracted most attention on the part of ethnologists and missionaries. Indeed the Nanabozho or Minabozho of the Algonquins has come to be regarded as a typical example of the kind of divinity in question.

The purpose of this chapter is not, however, to enter into detail, but to state the principle and to explain its essential meaning: it will thus be sufficient to begin by saying that the demiurge, who is also the hero who founds the material and spiritual civilization, and is thus inventor or discoverer, as well as initiator, appears in the form either of an animal or of a man or of some mysterious and indeterminate creature.[1] His myth is a series of acts or adventures, often grotesque and unintelligible, which constitute so many symbolical teachings, sometimes of esoteric significance. The demiurge may appear as a sort of emanation from the Creator; he has been described as the life which is incarnated in all beings, and thus he assumes all their possibilities, all their struggles, and all their destinies. There is something protean, chaotic, and absurd about him, and in him the Divine is combined with the tenebrous. To him has been attributed a desire for dissimulation and "occultation," and in this respect he appears like a wise actor who deliberately plays the fool;[2] his acts are incomprehensible, like the *koans* of Zen. It must be remembered that the bizarre and even the shocking often serve as a protective veil for the sacred, and this is the reason for the dissonances in revealed Scriptures and also, on a more outward level, for the grimacing monsters on the doors of sanctuaries.

In order to penetrate the enigma of the demiurge-buffoon, or to get to the very root of the enigma, one must have recourse to the Vedantic

---

1. The demiurge often appears as the "Great Hare." For the Sioux he is the "Spider"—a dethroned god, like Susano in Shinto—while for the Blackfeet he is the "Old Man," who becomes "Old Man Coyote" for the Crows. In Iroquois mythology the beneficent demiurge Teharonhiawagon has a twin brother, Tawiskaron, who incarnates the tenebrous aspect. The latter always seeks to imitate the former, but finishes by being killed by him after a terrible combat. It should be noted that for the Sioux the presence of Iktomi, the "Spider," does not alter the fact that the demon as such is Iya, the "Cyclone," and that the "culture hero" (*Kulturheros*) is a feminine divinity of luminous character, namely Pte San Win, the "White Buffalo." This means that in this mythology, as in certain others of the same type, the demiurgic function is incarnated in three or several personifications, depending on whether it is "passional," "tenebrous," or, on the contrary, "luminous." At all events, it is impossible to give an account of these shifting textures of symbolism in exhaustive terms or in a systematic manner, as long as one remains on the level of simple images.

2. It is this that causes certain Indians to say that the creator-initiator "disguises himself" as a crow, or a coyote, or a hare.

notion of *Māyā,* and also, secondarily, to the idea of the sacrifice of *Purusha. Māyā* comprises the three *gunas,* the three cosmic qualities or tendencies: the upward *(sattva),* the spreading or expansive *(rajas),* and the downward *(tamas).* The demiurge is firstly identified with primordial chaos, and then becomes the prototype of all things, both of good and of evil; the diversity and inequality of earthly creatures, ranging from the sublime to the nightmarish, attest this. As for *Purusha,* his fragmented body, passing from the celestial Substance to a sort of universal coagulation, has become the sum of all creatures, the good as well as the bad, some parts of his body pertaining to *sattva,* others to *rajas,* or to *tamas.*

The Semitic religions make a clear distinction between the personification of evil and the Sovereign Good; but the inverse perspective is not entirely absent from the theologies of these religions, since it is said that God "hardened the heart of Pharaoh," and one finds other things of this kind which, while obviously allowing of a metaphysical explanation—in that domain they arouse no question—nevertheless shock a certain "moral logic." The presence of the serpent in the Earthly Paradise is an analogous enigma, and likewise the pact which seems to exist between God and the devil on the subject of mankind: the devil has the right to seduce men, God "permits" evil without positively "willing" it. All these difficulties are clarified in the light of the doctrine of *Māyā.*

The key to this doctrine is basically that by definition Infinitude demands the dimension of the finite. It is the latter which, while "gloriously" manifesting the inexhaustible possibilities of the Divine Self, projects these right up to the limits of nothingness, if one may so express it. Nothingness "is" not, but it "appears" with respect to the real, as the real projects itself towards the finite. Now, to move away from the Divine Principle is to become "other than He," while remaining of necessity in Him, since He is the sole Reality. This means that the world necessarily comprises—in a relative fashion, of course, since nothingness does not exist—that privation of reality or of perfection which we call "evil." On the one hand, evil does not come from God, since being negative, it cannot have any positive cause; on the other, evil results from the unfolding of Divine manifestation, but in this respect, precisely, it is not "evil," it is simply the shadow of a process which is positive in itself. It is this that the myth of the demiurge-buffoon expresses in its fashion.

Finally, if we consider in *Māyā* the quality of "obscurity" or "ignorance" *(tamas)* as it is manifested in Nature in general or in man in particular, we are compelled to see in it what might be called the "mystery of absurdity"; the absurd is that which, in itself and not as regards its metaphysical cause, is deprived of sufficient reason and manifests no more than its own blind accidentality.[3] The genesis of the world in the first place, and then the unfolding of human events, appear as a struggle against absurdity; the intelligible is affirmed as a contrast to the unintelligible. Without this substance of incomprehensibility—of blind chance, even—there can be no world and likewise no soul; the soul is a microcosm, it obeys the same laws as the universe. Our prototype is Adam, "made in the image of God"; but that does not prevent our carrying within ourselves, as did this first image of God, all the absurdity of the Fall. The demiurge of Shamanism reminds us of this in its own way.

3. Sophocles' Antigone likewise shows us the crafty and incalculable character of a certain aspect of *Māyā,* and in this respect the gods do not differ from the playful and unintelligible semidivinities of North American Shamanism. We are here concerned with what the Hindus call *līlā,* the "Divine play." This play, in its lower modalities, is there to be overcome by the sage, and this victory coincides, precisely, with the higher modalities (perfectly intelligible since pertaining to *sattva)* of the same eternal and inexhaustible play. "Everything is absurd except God," so might one say in a certain sense, recalling that "everything is perishable except the Face of *Allāh.*"

The chaotic nature of the Red Indian demiurge, as well as the presence of the same characteristic in numerous Sacred Texts of the first importance, calls for a few remarks on the enigma of prophecies—something which is by no means unconnected with our subject. It is in a sense impossible that a prophecy which concerns, not a particular fact, but a complex of facts relating to the unfolding of the human cycle, should be absolutely exact and thus exhaust in advance the march of the future. What is changed or dissimulated, or even confused, in such cases, is not the facts insofar as essentials are concerned—this is obvious—but their order of succession and their proportions.[4] It is as if the prophecy were a shattered stained glass window, put together again without any regard for the logical placing of the fragments; the message is given, but the form is broken, for "only God knows the hour." This is to say that no complex prophecy can be taken literally, except for the essential facts and the general meaning of the process. God always reserves to Himself unforeseeable modalities, and if, on the one hand, He is bound by His word, He nevertheless, on the other hand, keeps a margin of freedom, the effects of which can be foreseen by none.[5]

There is even something analogous in the different religions which, inasmuch as they are revelations, correspond in a certain way to prophecies. Their very diversity proves that there is necessarily, in

---

4. It may happen that different events or personages merge into one by virtue of their identity of function, or that designations of persons and events only express analogies, and other ellipses of this kind.

5. The story of Narasinha, the fourth *Avatāra* of Vishnu, provides an example of this law: Hiranyakasipu, having obtained from Brahma the promise that he would be killed neither by day nor by night, nor by man nor by animal, thought that everything was permitted him, until Vishnu intervened in the form of a man with a lion's head—"neither man nor animal"—and killed the tyrant at the moment of dusk—"neither night nor day." Shakespeare took for his theme this subject, or this doctrine, in *Macbeth:* here, too, we find the same sequence of prophecy, false assurance, pride, and "Divine ruse" in the punishment.

PLATE IX

their appearance—but not in their essential content—an element which recalls, mutatis mutandis, what we may call the "jugglery" of the demiurge. This element does not appear from the point of view of each religion in itself—unless one opposes exoterism, considered as limitation, to esoterism which alone is absolutely true—but it appears from the point of view of the *religio perennis,* which penetrates all revelations and is not imprisoned in any. The sole Revealer, the Logos, plays with mutually irreconcilable forms, while offering one sole content of dazzling evidence.

ꓛ ꓛꓛ

This allusion to prophecies prompts the observation that there is a sort of absurdity which is purely apparent, and this is the accidental unintelligibility of wisdom, as, for example, it is described in the Koranic account of the meeting between Moses and Al-Khidr.[6] Here, according to the esoteric interpretation of the passage, the apparent absurdity is regarded as masking a dimension of depth which has no common measure with the platitudes of the profane world; it is an analogous sense that St. Paul speaks of true wisdom as "folly" in the eyes of the world. Since "extremes meet," the highest wisdom sometimes takes on the attitudes of its opposite; numerous stories of the saints bear witness to this. From a somewhat different point of view, it might be wondered what the meaning is of "practical jokers" such as Till Eulenspiegel or, among the Turks, Nasreddin Hoja. Perhaps the role of these jokers who became both popular and classic, or of the fictitious personages that correspond to them, is to exhaust the possibilities of absurdity contained in earthly *Māyā,* rather as the carnival seeks to neutralize subversive tendencies by deploying all the resources of

---

6. Sura, "The Cave," 63-82.

human imbecility.[7] But there is another very important aspect here, one which is related to the function of the court jester, and this is the right to utter or bring home truths which social convention tends to disguise, or, in a more general sense, to make people aware of the aspects of stupidity and "lack of imagination" indissociable from conventional life—in a word, to pierce its smug denseness by acting out scathing caricatures.[8]

Of a completely different order, at least intrinsically, is the apparent madness of the *heyoka* among the Sioux, and this brings us back to the question of hidden wisdom or the initiatory dissimulation of "pearls" before "swine": the *heyoka* were men who, having been honored in a dream by the vision of the Thunderbirds, had thereby contracted the obligation, on the one hand, to humble themselves, and, on the other, to dissimulate their consecration. Their case was similar, in certain respects, to that of the dervishes known by the name of the "people of blame" *(malāmātīyah)*, who sought to attract the reprobation of the profane and the hypocritical, while realizing inwardly the most perfect spiritual sincerity.[9] For the sake of humility the *heyoka* condemns himself henceforth to perform virtually all actions the wrong

---

7. In the Middle Ages, the feast of fools on New Year's Day gave rise to excesses of buffoonery which verged on sacrilege. A layman dressed up as a bishop gave the benediction and derisively proclaimed indulgences; people ate on the altar and played soldiers' games on it; the pseudo-bishop indulged in all manner of witticisms. Abuses like this show up a certain characteristic lack of equilibrium in the European mentality which has the tendency to go from one extreme to the other. It is true that the carnivalesque parodies had as their purpose the exhausting of the dangerous lower psychic possibilities in a harmless manner, but the fact that this was necessary and above all the excesses to which it gave rise prove the existence of a latent contradiction in the collective soul.

8. There is something of this in Omar Khayyam, who was, so to speak, the "court jester" of spirituality.

9. In the Christian world St. Benedict Labre was a very typical case of this kind. Here it is a question, not of a spiritual norm, but of vocation and of a very particular function.

way round, or to be a man "upside down"—for example, by pretending to shiver when it is hot, or to be stifled with heat when it is cold—and so to arouse the mockery of simple or mediocre people; nevertheless, he is considered to have received mysterious powers and may end by being deeply respected as a being apart and out of the common run, and no longer completely belonging to this world of rampant logic. Moreover—and this has already been alluded to—the behavior of the *heyoka* amounts to an initiatory language, comprehensible only to sages, as well as being a sacrificial vocation, that of being a "walking dead man" and called upon to reestablish inwardly the bridge between the world of matter and that of the spirit and immortality.

The Nanabozho of the Algonquins was no doubt the cosmic originator of good and evil, but he was also the first *heyoka* and the first "fool of God."

The Sun Dance

Theurgic phenomenology includes not only sacred symbols, supports of heavenly currents and subjective graces, but also and even above all, rites in which man actively cooperates with a saving theurgy. By "phenomenology" we simply mean the study of a category of phenomena, and not a particular philosophy which claims to resolve everything by observing or exploring in its fashion the phenomena that present themselves to one's attention, without being able to account for the central and ungraspable phenomenon that is the mystery of subjectivity; if we pause for a moment over this question, it is because our standpoint will provide a key to the theme we are proposing to discuss.

Scission into subject and object is the result of relativity: without this scission or polarity, there would be neither limitation nor diversity, and so no phenomenon. The subject can only grasp its own nature by recognizing it in the object and by discovering the object in itself, in the subject, which is the interiorized object just as the object is the exteriorized subject. The subject grasps its own reality in two ways, namely by reference to adequacy and by reference to totality: it grasps it adequately by and in the highest object to which human intelligence is proportioned, namely the absolute Object; and it grasps it totally by the contemplative assimilation of this Object, which implies the vacuity and extinction of the subject: vacuity from the point of view of the mental artifices which compromise the perception of the pure Object, and extinction from the point of view of the passional elements which limit and obscure the mirror that is the subject. It is in the coincidence between transcendent Object and pure subjectivity that the knowledge of the subject is realized, the subject which as such reveals a dimension of the Object, namely Consciousness; pure subjectivity is none other than the immanent Object, which reveals itself as absolute Subject, being objective only by reason of its veiling.

The transcendent Object, which by virtue of its absolute and infinite character awakens in the subject the consciousness of "immanent transcendence," if one may resort to such a paradoxical expression, may be the idea of the Absolute, of God, of the Great Spirit, but it may also be manifested in the form of a symbol, such as the sun. The sun is our macrocosmic heart, the heart is the sun of our microcosm; by knowing the sun—by knowing it in depth—we know ourselves. To know the Divine Object is to die for it and in it, so that it may be born in us; it is of this that the Sun Dance of the Indians of North America provides a striking example.

There are men who worship the sun because it is a manifestation of God; there are others who refuse to worship it because it is not God, which it seems to prove by the fact that it sets. The worshippers of the sun could assert with reason that it does not set, but that it is the rotation of the earth that creates this illusion; and their point of view could be compared to that of esoterism, which on the one hand is aware of the theophanic and as it were sacramental nature of the great phenomena of the visible world, and on the other hand knows the real and total nature of things and not a particular aspect or appearance only.

But a third possibility must also be mentioned, that of idolatry: there are men who worship the sun, not because they know that it manifests God, or that God manifests Himself through it, nor because they know that it is motionless and that it is not it that sets,[1] but because they imagine that God is the sun; in this case, the exoterists contemptuous of the sun may well cry paganism. They are relatively right, while being unaware that idolatry—or more precisely heliolatry—can only be a degeneration of a legitimate attitude; not, doubtless, an exclusive attitude, but in any case one that is conscious of the real situation, from the point of view of the subject as well as from that of the object.

Strictly speaking, the prostration in front of the Kaaba, or in the direction of the Kaaba, could be interpreted as an act of idolatry, seeing that God is outside space and that the Kaaba is a spatial and material object. If this reproach is absurd, the analogous reproach addressed to worshippers of the Principle "through" the sun, or the Christian, Hindu or Buddhist worshippers of icons, is so also, from the point of view of the principle and without taking account of differences of level that are always possible. One Sufi declared that the Kaaba revolved around him, the true Kaaba having been realized in his heart.

Like the Aryan mythologies—Hindu, Greco-Roman and Nordic— hyperborean Shamanism, to which the tradition, both differentiated and homogeneous, of the Indians of North America belongs, bears witness to a sacred interpretation of virgin Nature: this plays the role of

---

1. The fact that the sun, as far as one knows, moves in its turn does not come into consideration in a symbolism limited to our solar system.

Temple, as well as of Divine Book.[2] In this there is an element of esoterism—obviously so, since it is a question of a survival from the primordial religion—which monotheistic and Semitic exoterism had to exclude because it was obliged to oppose the naturalism of religions that had become pagan, but which, on the plane of the *religio perennis* or simply of truth as such, retains all its rights even within the framework of the Abrahamic monotheisms; for nothing can prevent Nature in general and its noble contents in particular—in spite of a certain omnipresent but altogether relative curse—from manifesting God and being the vehicle of graces, which they can communicate in certain conditions both objective and subjective.[3]

One example of these graces, which we intentionally take from Islam, because it is particularly abstract and iconoclastic, is the "mercy" *(rahmah)* which resides in rain, or which God sends by means of rain; the Prophet loved to bare his head to the rain because of the blessing of which it was the vehicle. The sun also transmits a blessing, but Islam does not make use of this, for reasons of perspective; in other words, the sun, in the consciousness of the Arabs, threatened to usurp the place of God. Altogether different is the perspective of the Hindus, who worship Surya, the male sun, or of the Japanese, whose worship is addressed to Amaterasu, the solar Goddess:[4] in these traditional

---

2. The Red Indians have the merit of always having been the defenders of Nature and of human solidarity with it. Their spokesmen declare today: "We do not wish equality, but the possibility of living our life; we refuse the way of the whites. Our values are founded on respect for Nature: according to us, man is possessed by the earth, not the earth by man."

3. Be that as it may, the Biblical injunction to "have dominion over the earth" does no more than define man; destined a priori for the Semitic nomads, it runs no risk of being misinterpreted—in the sense of a declaration of war against Nature—except in a European, Aristotelian and civilizationist climate.

4. The relationship between the sun and the tree—ritually actualized in the Sun Dance—occurs also in Shinto, according to which the primordial "pillar," joining Heaven and Earth and called "the ladder of Heaven," is the first of all created things; Amaterasu being, despite mythological fluctuations, the principal Divinity. This recalls the *Virgen del Pilar* at Saragossa: the Virgin—whose solar nature is emphasized by a halo of glowing rays—stands on a pillar of heavenly origin.

worlds, and in many others, man seeks to benefit from the solar power and possesses the means to do so.[5]

The great sacrificial Dance of the North American nomadic Indians, which is consecrated to the Solar Power, formerly included secondary rites that varied considerably according to the tribes: all sorts of mythological elements entered into its composition to such an extent in certain cases as to render the sun's role almost secondary. But this complexity, normal in a fragmented and shifting world like that of the Red Indians, is not of a nature to invalidate the fundamental content of the ritual cycle in question; this content has in fact survived all the political and religious tribulations which the Indians have had to suffer since the beginning of the 19th century.

Essentially the Sun Dance has two meanings, one outward and the other inward: the first is changing, the second invariable. The more or less outward intention of the Dance may be a personal vow, or the prosperity of the tribe; or again, more profoundly—with the Cheyenne for example—the desire to regenerate the entire creation.[6] The inward and invariable intention is to be united with the Solar Power, to establish a link between the Sun and the heart—in short, to realize a ray which attaches the earth to Heaven, or to reactualize this ray which is preexistent but lost. This strictly "pontifical" *(ponti-fex)* operation is based on the equation "heart-Sun": the sun is the Heart of the

---

5. For the Hindus, the *sauras* especially, the sun is the "Eye of the World"; according to the *Rigveda*, it is the soul "of things animate and inanimate," which is to say that it manifests the universal Substance, which is luminous and penetrates every thing. The rite of *sūryadarshana* consists of exposing newborn babies to the sun's rays for a moment, which indicates the benefic power of the solar star; a power which is actualized thanks to a conceptual and ritual system that permits this attitude or this worship.— Similarly, in North America, we have seen Indians stretch their arms towards the rising sun, and then rub their bodies so as to impregnate themselves with the strength of its rays.

6. This parallelism between a collective earthly intention and a personal heavenly intention manifests a particular aspect of the complementarity between exoterism and esoterism.

PLATE X

Macrocosm, the human heart is the sun of the microcosm that we are. The visible sun is only the trace of the Divine Sun, but this trace, being real, is efficacious and allows the operation of "analogical magic," so to speak.

The central element of the rite is the tree, image of the cosmic axis which joins earth to Heaven; the tree is the presence—necessarily vertical—of the Celestial Height over the terrestrial plane; it is what allows the contact, both sacrificial and contemplative, with the Solar Power. It is to this tree, chosen, felled, and set up ritually,[7] that the dancers in the old days were attached by thongs hooked into their chests; in our day the only element of the sacrifice that has always been retained is the fast, uninterrupted for the duration of the Dance—some three or four days—which symbolically and qualitatively is sufficient when one considers that the dancers must abstain from drinking in a torrid heat, while executing the prescribed movement for hours on end.[8]

This movement is a coming and going between the central tree and the circular shelter, covered with boughs; the dance can thus be likened to the two phases of breathing or to the beating of the heart; the entire sacred lodge, with the tree in the middle, is like a great heart whose vital phases are represented by the ebb and flow of the dance, and this symbolism is intensified by the beating of the drum and by the singing which recalls through its monotonous alternations the waves of the ocean. It is from the center that the dancers derive their strength: their withdrawal corresponds to the expansive phase—to the assimilation or the radiation—of the spiritual influence present in the tree.

---

7. See *The Sacred Pipe*, op. cit., the chapter "The Sun Dance." Cf. also *The Arapaho Sun Dance* (Chicago, Field Columbian Museum, 1903) and *The Ponca Sun Dance* (Chicago, Field Columbian Museum, 1905) by George A. Dorsey, studies which give an idea, at least, of the complex possibilities of the Dance with the differences of mythology and ritual that vary with each tribal tradition.

8. It still happens, however, that some Indians practice the rite in the ancient manner.

One might wonder how such a desire for spiritual realization accords with an adventurous and warrior way of life and with the resultant ruggedness of manners. It must be understood that for the Indian life "is what it is," which means that it is a texture of things and events, of forms and destinies, in which the outer man participates, performing and undergoing them according to the laws of Nature, but of which the inner man is independent and which he transcends and dominates in a certain manner; there is in this a fruitful combination of the veneration for impersonal Nature and the affirmation of the sacerdotal and heroic personality, and herein lies the foundation of Indian stoicism, which is the moral expression of this apparent antinomy.[9]

In approaching the central tree and then receding from it by small steps, without ever turning his back to it, the sacred dancer shakes an eagle plume in each hand while blowing, to the same rhythm, an eagle-bone whistle held in the mouth; the somewhat strident and plaintive sound thus produced is the equivalent of prayer or invocation; it reminds one of the cry of the eagle soaring in the immense solitude of space towards the sun. The dance is accompanied throughout by the singing of a group of men seated about a huge drum which they beat with vehemence in a rapid rhythm, thus emphasizing the virile character of their chant—song of victory and at the same time of nostalgia, victory over the earth and nostalgia for Heaven.[10] At sunrise a particular rite takes place: the dancers face the rising sun and—while

9. Shintoism presents the same complementariness between Nature-Object and Hero-Subject, each of the two poles recalling the mysteries of Transcendence and Immanence.

10. A victory which is at least symbolic, sacrificial and thus virtual; but really victorious just the same from a certain human point of view. Effective victory is a gift from heaven and not a human feat.

singing—greet it, with both arms outstretched towards it so as to become impregnated with the "Solar Power."

Throughout the Dance the central tree is charged with blessings; the Indians touch it and then rub their faces, bodies and limbs; or they pray to the Great Spirit while touching the tree; healings sometimes take place, prayers are answered and protection granted. Extraordinary phenomena of various kinds have been observed, sometimes visions, but above all a sensation of coolness in the proximity of the central tree, betokening the presence of benefic powers.

This idea of "power" is crucial for the Indian: the Universe is a texture of powers all emanating from one and the same Power which is subjacent and omnipresent, and at once impersonal and personal. For the Indians the spiritual man is united to the Universe or the Great Spirit by the cosmic powers which penetrate, purify, transform and protect him; he is simultaneously pontiff, hero and magician; around him, these powers are apt to manifest themselves through spirits, animals and the phenomena of Nature.

The Sun Dance is intended to become a permanent inner state: a decisive contact with the Sacramental Luminary has taken place; an indelible trace remains in the heart. The profane barrier between ordinary consciousness and the Immanent Sun is lifted, and the person lives hereafter under another sign and in another dimension.

The Sun Dance takes place once a year, in the summer, but it has its reflection or prolongation in the rites of the Sacred Pipe which are practiced in commemoration of the Dance at each full moon; these sessions comprise, along with the use of the eagle-bone whistles, prayers addressed to the four Directions of space, then to the Great Spirit, who both contains and projects this quaternity. The symbol for this metaphysic, as we have been told, is the cross inscribed in the circle: the terrestrial cross—with its North-South and East-West axes—and the celestial circle. At its extremities the horizontal cross touches Heaven; its center also touches Heaven through the axis Earth-Zenith, which is precisely what the Sun Dance tree represents.

This symbolism recalls another sacral image—that of the Feathered Sun, which is found on buffalo hides used as cloaks and occasionally as a background for ceremonies. The Sun is composed of concentric circles formed of stylized eagle feathers; the resulting impression is particularly evocative in that the symbol simultaneously suggests center, radiation, power and majesty. This symbiosis between the sun and the eagle, which is to be found again in the celebrated headdress of feathers formerly worn by chiefs and great warriors, brings us back to the symbolism of the Sun Dance: here man is spiritually transformed into an eagle soaring towards Heaven and becoming identified with the rays of the Divine Sun.

A Message on Indian Religion

 We are told that the Indians of former times were a very religious people, and there can be no doubt that this was so, and that it is so even today to a large extent. Today, the old religion and Christianity exist side by side; some think they are opposed and others think that in their deep meaning they are not; if there is any opposition, it can only be on a superficial level. Rather than discuss this matter, I shall answer the following question, the most important of all: What is religion? What is its essential nature?

There are two things to be said. First, religion is essentially discernment. It is discernment between God and the world, between the Real and the unreal, or between the Everlasting and the ephemeral. Secondly: religion is union. It is union with God, the Great Spirit. Everything in religion has its foundation in one of these two elements:

Translator's note: This text was written for a group of Indian friends.

in discernment or in union. Man is intelligence and will, and religion is discernment and concentration.

If we consider the old Indian religion, we must first state that it is subject to many variations due to the scattering of the tribes; but there is nevertheless a unity based on the symbolism of the Directions of Space and on the use of the Sacred Pipe, and above all on the idea of a Supreme Being. And this religion too, with its many forms and its many different symbols is firstly discernment and then union—discernment between this vanishing world of dreams and the everlasting Reality which lies behind it, and union with this Reality even on this earth and in this life.

If the Indians stated that God was the sun or a tree, they would be pagans. But the oldest statements prove that the authorities of the Indian religion never assumed that. God is one, but He has many manifestations. So the Indians are no pagans.

If some would object that Indian individuals could have been pagans by lack of understanding of their own religion, the same would be equally true of Christians or followers of other faiths. The ancient peoples around the Jews were pagans, except for a few sages among them; but it does not follow from this that the Indian religion is heathen. It could be so by utter lack of understanding, but it is not so for those who understand it.

The angle of vision, of course, is different from that of Christian theology; it is more related to the outlook of Asian peoples. Like the Asian, the American Indian is much concerned with the question of the spiritual meaning of Nature. To see God only in Nature would be false, for He is essentially above all form; but He manifests Himself also through natural forms. The Great Spirit is not the Sun, the Eagle, the Buffalo or the Rock, but these forms are something of Him, and He may be reached through them, and even seen in them, or behind them.

PLATE XI

The Great Spirit is the innermost Self of all creatures.

The question has been asked whether the ancient Indians called God "Great Spirit" or not. It is obvious that not all of them did; it is certain that some did; howbeit, there is no doubt that this term is very convenient for the Indian idea of God, for the following reason: the Indians conceive God simultaneously in His unity and in His diversity, and therefore they speak of many "Spirits"; in another language, these may be called Angels or, on the highest level, Divine Qualities; earthly Spirits—which are below the Angels—may be meant also, or more accurately: those earthly Spirits who reflect the Angels and thus the Divine Qualities. It is like a sun ray which, though being pure light, changes its color along its way. But all these aspects are essentially one, and therefore we may speak of the "Great Spirit," an expression which recalls the distinction between diversity and unity in the Divine Reality. The Indian idea of God is neither anthropomorphic nor pantheistic, it is polysynthetic, metaphysically speaking.

The most important manifestations of the Great Spirit are the West, the North, the East, the South, Heaven and Earth; then come forms like the Sun, the Eagle, the Buffalo, the Rock, the Morning Star. Firstly, all these phenomena are physical things, which we can see and feel. Secondly, they represent Principles which act everywhere in the whole Universe. Thirdly, these Principles act in the human soul: in every soul there is a West, a North, an East, a South, a Heaven, an Earth, a Sun, an Eagle, a Buffalo, a Rock and so on. Fourthly, they are prefigured in the Great Spirit Himself: although He is One, He has in Himself all these Qualities whose outer form we see in the Directions of Space and in certain phenomena of Nature.

The Great Spirit is the hidden Reality of all things. There are two truths to combine: in one sense, He is infinitely above us and we are totally other than Him, and in another sense, He is within us and He is nearer to us than we ourselves are.

The Indians have the Sacred Pipe and the Sweat Lodge; they also have the solitary Invocation and the Sun Dance. These may be considered as the main features of the Plains Indian religion. There are other very important rites, but as the number four is sacred with the Indians, we mention only these four most important forms of worship.

The Sacred Pipe means prayer. With it, man prays not only for himself, but also for the whole Universe. The whole Universe prays with him.

The Sweat Lodge means purification. In it, man renews himself; he becomes a new being. He becomes pure before his Creator.

The solitary Invocation is the highest form of prayer. It is contemplation and union. But it also benefits the whole community, in a subtle and indirect way. This solitary Invocation should be continued even in daily life; it should become unceasing prayer. For that, a traditional Indian name of the Great Spirit may be invoked within the heart. This is the highest and most complete form of spiritual life.

The Sun Dance is in a sense the prayer of the whole community. For those who dance, it is union with the Great Spirit. Afterwards, the Sun Dance should continue as a spiritual vibration in the heart. It is a symbol of our connection with God. If the Divine Presence dwells in our heart, we are attached to God by a golden ray. In the Sun Dance, we are like an eagle flying towards the Sun; like him, we are above earthly things, in the pure air of the high mountains, and in holy loneliness with our Creator. The Sun Dance attaches us to the Great Spirit; those who have attended it can never forget it.

The writer of these lines is not an Indian, but he has attended two Sun Dances inside the Sacred Lodge, fasting the second day with the Indians. He has been adopted by the Sioux tribe and received the name "Bright Star" *(Wicahpi Wiyakpa)*. He knows well certain holy Traditions of Asia and he accepts every true and traditional religion, but for this very reason he knows the modern white civilization to be an error, which has nothing to do with Christianity; this deviated and unnatural civilization is contrary to Christianity as well as to every true religion. The writer of these lines knows that the present world will come to an end, in a future which is not far off. He thinks that nothing which is really spiritual must be lost. We must cling to the holy Name of God and trust in it, whatever its traditional form may be.

Never forget that religion is discernment between the Everlasting and the ephemeral, and union with the Everlasting. In other words, religion is basically discernment and concentration; separation from evil, which is illusion, and union with the Divine Good, which is Truth and eternal Reality.

Many people think that magic is an essential element of Indian religion. This is not so, for magic is only a science or an art; religion can exist without magic, of course. Magic in itself is neither good nor bad, it is amoral. Magic performed in the name of the Great Spirit and with the help of good Spirits, and for good purposes, may be called "white magic"; the same art performed without appeal to the Great Spirit and with the help of bad spirits and for evil purposes, may be called "black magic" or sorcery. Sorcery has always been strongly forbidden everywhere, and it very often harms the sorcerer himself even in this life.

White magic (the *yuwipi* of the Lakota) becomes dangerous if it is considered as self-sufficient, exactly as it is dangerous to pray only for earthly advantages. We are allowed to pray for everything which is helpful to us, provided that we pray as well and even more for our immortal souls: we must pray for virtue and spiritual knowledge and eternal life, and for union with the Great Spirit, and also for the welfare of the community to which we belong and for God's final victory over all evil.

This victory is certain, but prayer purifies the heart; the Great Spirit likes man's prayers, He wishes us to pray. The best prayer is His Sacred Name, which contains all other possible prayers. But as long as we use many words to pray for our body, we must also use many words to pray for our soul. Besides this and above all, let us pray for God's sake, invoking His Name alone, from the depth of our heart, just as a bird sings without wanting anything other than God's glory.

His Holiness and the Medicine Man

It happened during my first visit to the Red Indians of the North American Plains, ten years ago.* A spiritual encounter between His Holiness the Jagadguru and a Red Indian holy man has taken place, through the medium of a picture of His Holiness and a prayer of the Red Indian.

It came about in this way: I was in Sheridan in the state of Wyoming, with my travelling companion, during the All Indian Days; one morning while walking across an open space where the tents or tipis of many Red Indians of different tribes were pitched, we heard a voice which seemed to be calling us; we went in that direction and approached one of the tents, asking if somebody had called us and

* Translator's note: This short article was Schuon's contribution to the Jubilee volume *Sankara and Shanmata* (Madras, India, 1969), brought out in honor of the Jagadguru of Kanchipuram.

were told that they had. An old man was there, and a younger woman with some children also present. The old man wanted to know where we came from and who we were, and we told him everything and began to talk about spiritual matters and about the ancient American Indian religion. The old man explained that they were Cheyenne Indians; he spoke about the Sun Dance and said: "Our religion is the same as what is in the Holy Scriptures; God—the Great Spirit—cannot be seen, He is pure Spirit."

"The Sun and the Earth," he added, "are not gods, but they are like Father and Mother to us; and all the things of Nature, such as streams and rocks, are holy."

He told us that he was a very important priest of the Cheyennes, the so-called "Keeper of the Sacred Arrows"; these are the holy objects of the Cheyenne tribe. They are marvelously beautiful, the old man said, but they are always hidden in a sacred bundle, which is opened only on very few occasions. We were told that these Arrows had been brought to his tribe some thousand years ago; that they had been brought by a "Spirit Man," who was transparent; and that the whole tribe witnessed the event at that remote time. The Spirit Man said: "As long as you keep these Arrows, your people will not disappear; if you lose them, the rivers and the grass will dry up." And the old priest added: "Maybe this would mean the end of the world."

Then I showed him some pictures I had with me; one was the image of His Holiness the Jagadguru of Kanchipuram. I spoke to the old Cheyenne priest about Hinduism and explained to him who His Holiness was. He took the picture in one hand and raised the other hand towards the sky; this is the Red Indian's gesture of prayer. He prayed a long time, always looking at the picture; and after a while he put his hand on it and then rubbed his face and his breast with the hand, in the Indian way, to impregnate himself with the Jagadguru's blessing. At last he kissed the picture with fervor; during the whole scene, I also prayed inwardly with him, and so did my companion.

PLATE XII

A few years after this meeting, we heard that the Cheyenne holy man—Last Bull was his name—had passed away.

One of my friends then visited His Holiness the Jagadguru and gave him a book on Red Indian religion called *The Sacred Pipe*;[1] and His Holiness, after having read it, pointed out that the rites of the Red Indians present striking analogies with certain Vedic rites.

A few words should be said here about this ancient American religion, or more precisely that of the Plains and Woodland Indians. The most eminent manifestations of the "Great Spirit" are the Cardinal Points together with Zenith and Nadir, or with Heaven and Earth, and next in order are such as the Sun and the Morning Star. Although the Great Spirit is One, He comprises in Himself all those qualities the traces of which we see and the effects of which we experience in the world of appearances. The East is Light and Knowledge and also Peace; the South is Warmth and Life, therefore also Growth and Happiness; the West is fertilizing Water and also Revelation speaking in lightning and thunder; the North is Cold and Purity, or Strength. Thus it is that the Universe, at whatever level it may be considered, whether of Earth, Man or Heaven, is dependent on the four primordial determinations: Light, Heat, Water, Cold.

A most striking feature of the North American branch of the Primordial Sanatana Dharma is the doctrine of the four yugas: the sacred animal of the Plains Indians, the buffalo, symbolizes the *mahāyuga*, each of its legs representing a yuga. At the beginning of this *mahāyuga* a buffalo was placed by the Great Spirit at the West in order to hold back the waters which menace the earth; every year this bison loses a

---

1. Op.cit.

hair, and in every yuga it loses a foot. When it will have lost all its hair and its feet, the waters will overwhelm the earth and the *mahāyuga* will be finished. The analogy with the bull of Dharma in Hinduism is very remarkable; at every yuga, this bull withdraws a foot, and spirituality loses its strength; and now we are near the end of the *kali-yuga*. Like the orthodox Hindus, the traditional Red Indians have this conviction, which is obviously true in spite of all the mundane optimism of the modern world; but let us add that the compensation of our very dark age is the Mercy of the Holy Name, as it is emphasized in the *Manava-Dharma Shastra* and the *Shrimad Bhagavata* and other holy scriptures.

All this may give the impression of a rather singular contribution in honour of His Holiness the Jagadguru; but it is in reality not so unrelated, and this for three main reasons: firstly, it is certainly a great event that, for the first time in history, a Red Indian holy man manifests his love for a Hindu holy man; secondly, this apparently small incident reminds us of the unity of the Primordial Sanatana Dharma, which is more or less hidden beneath the many forms of intrinsically orthodox Tradition; and this unity is especially represented by the very function of the Jagadguru, who incarnates the Universal Truth. Thirdly, this little incident marking a symbolical encounter between a Red Indian priest and a Hindu priest was in fact an act of prayer; and it shows us that in prayer all earthly differences such as space and time are transcended, and that in prayer we are all united in one state of purity and in one perfume of Deliverance.

PART TWO

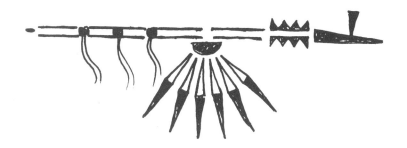

Excerpts From a Diary

Journeys to America

Journey to America–1959

AMONG THE LAKOTA

We went to a place shaded by trees where there were many Indians singing, drumming and dancing, men and women all in full costume. We met Red Shirt, whose acquaintance we had made in Brussels;[1] he introduced us to a grandson of Red Cloud—the younger one—who then took us both by the hand and led us into the circle of dancers; there he made a short speech in Lakota to introduce us to the Sioux. Then all sang a greeting song and my wife had to join in the dance with them; after this Red Cloud's grandson (Charles) took us to his

---

1. The Schuons met a group of Sioux when they attended the 1958 World's Fair, held in Brussels, Belgium.

elder brother, to whom we presented my painting of the White Buffalo Cow Woman; the old man studied it carefully and after a while remarked that at that time the Pipe was still made from the bone of a deer, there were not yet any Pipes made of wood and stone.

The whole morning I sat beside Chief Red Cloud, (James) the eldest grandson of the great chief. He recounted to me, with many slow gestures, something of the history of his tribe and explained how all the vast land around used to belong to the Lakota, how everything had been taken from them, and how Big Foot's band had been "rubbed out" at Wounded Knee. When I was alone with him, I communicated to him the essential of what I have to say to the Indians; he nodded in ready agreement, then for a long time we remained silent. At length I said to him—for he intends soon to go to Washington—that one must insist that the Lakotas be given work on their own land, and not somewhere far away. Again we were silent for a long time. All at once he asked for a piece of paper and wrote a few words in Lakota on it; he then told me that he wished to adopt me as his brother and call me Wambali Ohitika (Brave Eagle) and my wife Onpahi Ske Win (Antelope Teeth Woman); antelope teeth, which are very precious for the Indians, correspond to our pearls.

I had to think of *Black Elk Speaks*, as Chief Red Cloud sat beside me on a grassy rise, with his gray braids and his wide-brimmed black felt hat adorned with beadwork and feathers—as with gestures of the hands he conjured up the old days, and pointing towards the dance ground before us, said: "At that time, there were soldiers everywhere here."

When we were taken to see Chief Red Cloud for the first time, he more than once cast a searching, penetrating glance at me. Then suddenly he seemed to conceive a great confidence in me; this I could see quite plainly. Once he put on his wonderful leather shirt, adorned with long fringes and embroidered here and there in red, and held a fan of eagle feathers in his hand; in his hair he wore a long feather, like his famous grandfather.

Before night came, we had a long talk with One Feather[2] and his wife. Tradition was dying out everywhere, he said, but there were men who sought to keep it alive. Before the coming of the white man, the Indians had the religion of the Pipe, and this had been brought to them just as the Ten Commandments had been brought to the whites. But with his religion the white man had also introduced the devil. One devil was alcohol, another was money. Christ had been crucified, but the Indians crucified themselves on the cottonwood tree; the cross of Christ had been of oak, whereas the Sun Dance Tree was, precisely, the cottonwood; a cross section through any branch of this tree always showed a golden star.

When One Feather speaks of spiritual things, he becomes a completely different man; he then speaks slowly and softly, becomes solemn, and emphasizes his words with impressive gestures. His tremendous angular and sharply chiseled face, with the triangular eyes, then becomes altogether spiritual.

At one point One Feather said: "What can never be taken from a man is his upbringing; it can neither be taken away nor sold. Everyone must discipline his character and shape his personality. If one lets one-

---

2. One Feather was one of the Sioux the Schuons met at the World's Fair in Brussels.

self go, one falls and bears the responsibility for it." This is a truly Indian way of seeing things.

At last we arrived in Keystone, high in the Black Hills, and here we found Ben Black Elk.[3]

It was an unforgettable evening: Black Elk and One Feather sang incessantly, drumming all the while—sometimes their wives sang along with them—and finally the Sacred Pipe was placed on the ground and the Pipe Song was sung; for this all the lights were put out, as in a session of *yuwipi*. Then the lights were lit again and the Pipe was passed round; prayers were said. Ben explained, among other things, that the distinctive sign of the Indian religion was the circle with the cross within it.

We spoke of Indian names: Tatanka Iyotake, said Ben, did not mean "Sitting Bull" but "The Buffalo That Takes Possession," that is, that protects the cows and the calves; Tashunka Witko did not mean "Crazy Horse" but "Spirit Horse"—the horse, filled with the spirit, that leaps about like a colt.

As we passed a wide valley opening that cut through a long mountain ridge, One Feather said: "That is the Buffalo Gap. It was through this door that the buffalo herds used to come streaming in. Just as the Great Spirit has made a Door through which man can attain to Him, so He has made a Door through which the buffaloes come to man." This has a deep significance, when one remembers that the buffalo is at once primordial Ancestor, Revealer, Nourisher and Word of God.

One Feather also said: "You cannot make yourself a medicine man. An old medicine man must first of all tell you: 'You can become a med-

---

3. Son of the famous medicine man Hehaka Sapa (Black Elk).

icine man.' You must receive a consecration from an elder."

Perhaps in order to draw attention to the similarity between the Christian cross and the Indian directions of space, One Feather said: "When a man is a Catholic or an Episcopalian, he hangs his cross around his neck; but when an Indian smokes the Pipe, he turns towards the Four Directions and towards Heaven and Earth, and then he must be mindful of his mouth, his actions and his character." He also said that if someone really wished to learn sacred chants, he must fast for four days in the solitude of the hills.

One Feather had originally wanted to be trained to be a medicine man, but because he had gone to school and thought he knew more than his grandfather, he could not become a medicine man: "Because I thought I knew more, I fell." His brother did not have this prejudice and so obtained permission to become a medicine man; but he is not ready yet.

Something that Ben Black Elk had explained to us occurs to me at this moment: the Indians do not worship rocks, trees and animals; but because man was created after all the other creatures, it is only through these creatures that he can approach God. Which means that just as for others a Book or a God-man is symbol and mediator, so for the Red Indians the whole of Nature is symbol and mediator.

Yesterday in Allen[4] we were again struck by the fascinating beauty of many of the Indian faces. There was a boy who resembled a child

---

4. South Dakota, near the Pine Ridge Reservation.

Pharaoh or a Mayan prince; he was uncannily beautiful and had super-naturally mysterious eyes; he made me think of an *Avatāra*. Sitting next to my wife was a little girl who looked like a Balinese; she chatted with my wife and danced behind her in the big circle. Many grown-up girls also struck us, each one a model of Mongolian beauty; I should also like to mention a youth whose dancing was among the most remarkable performances of this art that I have ever seen.

"The cottonwood tree," said Red Cloud IV (Edgar) to us this morning, "does not rot and is never eaten away. Its leaf is the model for our tipis and our moccasins. Inside it is the Morning Star." Thereupon he picked up a branch and cut it across, and the pith star appeared.

He also said that on no account did he want to be buried under the earth, but on a scaffold in the open air, like his forefathers. The churchmen were of course against this but could do nothing to prevent it.

Pointing to some sunflowers, he said that the Indians painted these flowers on their breasts for the Sun Dance, because they always turn towards the sun.

This evening we were to attend a magic healing ceremony in Oglala,[5] but the medicine man, Poor Thunder, has gone to the Arapahos; he usually heals by means of owl spirits. There was some talk of Good Lance—another medicine man—taking over the healing with his songbird spirits, but now he too is unavailable. At all events we had been warned not to have any metal on us during the magic

---

5. South Dakota, on the Pine Ridge Reservation.

PLATE XIII

session; the spirits would rush upon the metal objects and break them to pieces. People who only half believed in spirits or who did not believe in them at all would get their heads wrapped up in blankets.

The work of Black Elk is alive, it lives on, but the Indians, true to their nature, keep it more or less secret. When one speaks with Indians about spiritual matters, one must take great care to choose the right moment, then to speak little and to frame properly what one says; in between one must speak of birds and trees. In general the Indians have a pronounced feeling for reality, for true proportions; they abhor anything false—that is, removed from reality—or any unseemly chatter; but speaking with intensity is also foreign to them, unless it be on important occasions; nowadays, however, it is scarcely possible to speak about subtle spiritual matters on important occasions; that would be incompatible with the spiritual sensitivity of the Indians. There have, moreover, always been secret societies among them, and nowa-days, indeed, the secrecy is transferred to everything that is sacred, with certain exceptions; it is hard to draw a clear line here; where the line is drawn varies from case to case.

AMONG THE ABSAROKA

In the evening, supper in the Crows' camp. All the tipis are up now, their long poles standing out brightly illuminated against the night sky. We take our meal beside the beautifully decorated tipi of the Yellowtails, in a kind of arbor; each of us is given an enormous piece of meat.

Supper with our Crow friends—hard dried meat and raw vegetables; then a general dance. Around the fire, the dancing goes on—in a tremendously powerful and self-assured manner—the whole evening until midnight; a few Cheyennes also take part in it. My wife dances with the women; a beautiful, tall, very tastefully dressed girl is also there, her feet never seem to touch the ground; she is the granddaughter of the famous White Man Runs Him.[6]

In the night sky we see a magnificent aurora borealis, greenish and radiant, and undulating gently like a veil.

Among the Crows and Cheyennes, many children and young girls, as well as youths, have the same bewitching beauty as the young Sioux. With age this beauty changes its mode, that is to say, it is replaced by another, namely the old-age beauty of the Indian. The frequency of pure Far Eastern types is striking.

Journey with the Crow friends into the Bighorn Mountains to the famous Medicine Wheel, a gigantic wheel of stones set in the ground; it is an exact image of the Sun Dance Lodge. The origin of the sanctuary is unknown. In the evening the aged Real Bird told me there are three such monuments.

Conversation with the Yellowtails (Thomas and Susie). The downfall of the Indians, they say, can in part be accounted for by the fact that too many Indians have given up their old religion. They tell the story of a woman who died a few years ago, and who suddenly

---

6. One of Custer's Crow scouts.

returned to life and said that the place where she now lived was wonderful, that there could not be a more beautiful place, and that the Indians must hold fast to their old religion; as a proof that this was true, she said that such and such would soon happen; then she died again, and her predictions came true.

On the way home Yellowtail stops at a house and introduces to us one of his two brothers, an elderly man with an oval Mongolian face and the old hair style of the Crow: three braids—one on the back of his head—and high-brushed hair. This man, who only speaks broken English, is very friendly to us and expresses the hope that he will see us again at the All Indian Days in Sheridan.

This morning: conversation with Yellowtail about the Indian mystery societies and their strictly secret character. The rites occasionally carried out in front of white men or noninitiated Indians are always mere fragments of the real rites.

In the neighborhood of Fort Hall[7] the road turned off to the side; a large, white zigzag line, no doubt representing lightning, was painted on the ground, to show the Indians the way to the site of the Sun Dance. Upon arrival we stopped at the tipi of the sponsor, where we were received with friendly words by his wife and introduced to several Indians, including some venerable old men. We came to one of the festival shades made of branches—they reminded me of the Jewish Feast of Tabernacles—and here too we were introduced to several peo-

---

7. Idaho, on the Shoshoni-Bannock Reservation.

ple; over the entrance to this shade hung a stuffed eagle, with its wings outspread. The women were preparing the evening meal; the men sat round about, talking or remaining silent. A few people of mixed blood were present; as well as noble and refined faces, there were also some of crude and sinister appearance, as well as handsome figures there were also some that were coarse and overweight; some people had braids and high, broad-brimmed hats adorned with bead-work and feathers. Profound gravity and peasant-like jesting went hand in hand.

In the evening, after we had moved into the lodging that the sponsor of the Sun Dance put at our disposal—a gesture we could not refuse—we returned to the Sun Dance grounds; a fire had been lit, and there was vigorous drumming and singing in fierce and stirring tones; two men in the Sun Dance costume, their torsos bare, eagle-bone whistles in their mouths, stood there and now and then moved forward, while from their whistles they drew forth a shrill, plaintive sound; between times, speeches were made in the Shoshoni language.

THE SUN DANCE

When we arrived today at the site of the Sun Dance—a flat, desert-like piece of high ground—the Indians were in the course of erecting the sacred Tree; when it was up, they built the Lodge that surrounds the Tree, and provided it with green branches all round, to make a kind of shade-giving wall.

Yesterday evening Yellowtail became quite solemn; he had put on the Sun Dance costume: round his hips was a blanket, held in place by a wide belt; round his forehead was a beaded headband, with strings of beads that hung down over his temples; on one side of the headband were two large, white plumes; on his breast was the eagle-bone whistle. He was completely concentrated, drank for the last time before his three-day fast, spoke little and quietly; his wife was in the same state; she gave us a few final instructions, then went out of the tipi with her husband.

The opening of the Sun Dance was one of the most powerful things I have ever witnessed. We stood near the entrance of the Sun Dance Lodge among many Indians. After a while came the sun dancers, men and a few women, and twice went round the Lodge in opposite directions; in single file, one group went round from left to right and at the same time the others—crossing the first—went round from right to left; then they all entered the Lodge. In the darkness an extraordinarily powerful, rapid drumming began, and at the same time a monotonous, wild and thrilling singing; it was like a war cry, and yet was not of this world.

After some time, a fire was lit inside the Lodge; the Sun Dance Tree, brightly illuminated and golden, stood out against the very clear, star-studded night sky; opposite us, on the eastern side, hung the aforementioned eagle with the outspread wings, and on the other side of the Tree, facing the west, hung an uncanny, shaggy buffalo head. The sacred Tree was forked; where the trunk divided, a large bundle of sacred willow shoots was fastened, and the twelve cross beams forming the roof of the Lodge also met here. At the top of the Tree fluttered two ribbons, one yellow and one white—one for Heaven and one for Earth.

In the crowd we saw some very impressive and wonderful faces: for example, an old chief with aristocratic and stone-like countenance; at first he was standing in front of me, giving directions in a loud voice. Beside us stood an elderly woman, whose half intent, half sleep-like, prototypically Indian face was like the quintessence of everything Indian, a combination of rock and lightning; with half shut, unfathomable eyes she looked unwaveringly at the sacred Tree. The consonance of all these impressions—the Sun Dance Tree under the starry sky, the flickering fire, the thunderous drumming, the powerful singing, whose melody cascaded from high to low, the wonderful and timeless figures and faces—resulted in a truly grand and majestic image, indeed as powerful a one as senses or imagination can grasp.

At a certain moment, when a signal was given, we spectators all entered the Sun Dance Lodge and stood there near the fire; Deernose[8] had come with us; he explained some things to us and as it were acted as our guide. The old chief stood right beside the fire, in such a way that the flickering, glowing light emphasized still further the cold and rigid power of his spiritualized countenance.

Soon thereafter we went home, to allow ourselves a few brief hours of rest before morning, since we wished to be present for the greeting of the rising sun; at a little after four o'clock in the morning we came back to the Sun Dance mound. There, on the bare plain in the light of dawn, stood the Lodge, woven round with leafy branches; from the dark interior there resounded a drumming that made me think of galloping spirit-horses, and all the while the same powerful, magical singing rang out. The fire was still burning; following instructions we had received the evening before, we entered the Lodge and seated ourselves at the right-hand side of the entrance on the rush-covered ground. When at last the sun rose, all the dancers stood there in rows to greet it; with eagle-bone whistles in their mouths, they welcomed the gilding rays of the sun with a kind of shrill, thin, plaintive sound, reminiscent partly of an eagle's cry and partly of Japanese flutes; the two leaders—the sponsor and the medicine man—held their arms outstretched towards the sun. Then they all sat down, only the sponsor remained standing beside the Tree, praying long and fervently in Shoshoni; he then sat down and they sang softly. At length there was an interval, and Yellowtail came over and spoke a few words with us; thereafter we returned to our lodgings.

---

8. Donald Deernose, brother-in-law of Thomas Yellowtail.

PLATE XIV

On the barren, sandy and slightly undulating ground where the Sun Dance takes place stand the Trees of earlier Sun Dances; one of them still bears the bundle of willow shoots in its fork. An Indian woman had told us that this desolate, sandy ground had been deliberately chosen because this was fitting for the sacrifice; the earth too must be poor and must fast.

In the morning it was cold, and the dancers were wrapped in their blankets; when the sun rose, they let their blankets fall, allowing their torsos to be gilded by the reddish rays. In each hand they held an eagle plume, and with this they stroked their bodies, as if they wished to preserve the sun's blessing. At the same time they looked into the sun with half shut eyes, and tears ran down the cheeks of one of them.

Afternoon: the Dance sometimes rises to an extraordinary intensity; then the dancers move towards the Tree, forwards and back, sounding their eagle-bone whistles. Each whistle is ornamented with a white plume; and in each hand the dancer holds another white plume, waving it up and down; the circle surges forwards and backwards, dust rises, and the sun is high in the sky; the rapid, onrushing drumming thunders like a transporting magic. Beside the ten drummers sit a few women who wave green branches; their singing is drowned by the wild and hoarse singing of the men—singing that sounds like the howling of the wind or like battle cries, and yet is sacred like a timeless stream. Fresh sage gives off a wonderful scent, imparting to the consecrated place something pure and virginally paradisal.

A few aged Indian women are taking part in the Dance; one of them is as old as the hills and can scarcely walk, but despite her ninety-three years she is fasting, and she moves painfully forwards and back.

At day's end the setting sun is greeted; one dancer after another stands by the Tree, touches the trunk, prays inwardly, strokes the trunk and the mounded earth around it with the plumes—the medicine man does it with an eagle feather—and then strokes his arms and body with them.

The clear symbolical significance and the elemental convincing power of the Sun Dance are quite overwhelming. The Tree is the axis, and this is in our heart; the various elements of our soul revolve around this axis, moving backwards and forwards in exteriorization and interiorization, discrimination and union.

On the Tree hangs the buffalo head, adorned with sprigs of sage, facing the sunset, and also the eagle facing the sunrise; the sprigs of sage hang down beneath the buffalo's eyes. The buffalo is the sacred, primordial power and fecundity of the earth, and the eagle is the light that comes from above, the Revelation; the buffalo is mountain or rock, and the eagle sky and lightning; but the buffalo is also the sun, or the earthly image thereof.

The Sun Dance is the remembrance of God, purification from the multiple and the outward, union with the One and the Real.

Second day of the Sun Dance. We are also fasting. In the early morning, before sunrise, we are already in the sacred Lodge. Coming down the road in the half-light of dawn, one can hear from afar the drumming and the powerful singing.

After the greeting of the sun, the fire is allowed to die out; the dancers crouch around the embers, wrapped in their blankets and with heads bowed; they sing four songs, and after each song they blow their eagle-bone whistles four times; four is the sacred number of the Indians, deriving from the Four Directions of space, or the four quarters of the universe. These songs are altogether peaceful, rather like laments, and are sung with a restrained voice.

Today, the second day, the Sun Dance reached its dramatic climax. This second day is the most important one, it is like the heart of the sacred event. Most of the dancers had painted themselves, which gave some of them a ghostly appearance. Their torsos were yellow, and most of them had their faces daubed with white and red spots; a few of the men had encircled their eyes with red, to make it easier to look into the sun; Yellowtail had black zigzag lines on his upper arms. The semicircle where the dancers were was now turned into a closed corridor, roofed over with little fir trees; the white cloth that shut off the corridor from the drummers and the spectators could be raised like a curtain, so that the stakes became visible. It was between these stakes that the painted dancers now stood; then the powerful drumming started up again and the dancers moved forwards and backwards, incessantly blowing their eagle-bone whistles. We sat on the rush-covered ground beside the drummers in a crowd of Indians, both men and women; during the dancing every woman received a spray of willow shoots and waved it up and down, or from side to side, in time with the drumming. At this point sick people came and stood beside the Tree in the center; the medicine man—a Ute—did various things in order to transmit to them the healing blessing of the Tree; he held handfuls of leaves over their heads and stroked them with them, blew upon the sick people, worked on them with a fan of eagle feathers, and did other things of the kind.

The Sun Dance is a cosmic drama, indeed it is a cosmos in itself. It is without beginning and without end: it is the temporal fraction of a timeless and supernatural reality; it is as if it had fallen into time; in it everything becomes timeless, outward happening stands still. The rhythm of the drum is rhythm as such; all is rhythm and center, equilibrium and presence.

If the word "art" is appropriate here, one could say that the Sun Dance is a powerful work of art; at all events, one can understand why the Red Indians never felt the need to create a great epic or the like. The manner in which they saw and experienced Nature excluded precisely every kind of fine art.

In some of the Indians the Sun Dance seems to have become crystallized; it gives them a definitive stamp—it has in a way become congealed in them, or rather, they in it. Or again, it continues to vibrate in them, its rhythm is their life.

Sometimes venerable Indians come up to me, shake my hand, and look long and deep into my eyes.

Third day of the Sun Dance. Once more we went at earliest dawn to the flat mount, heard the drumming and singing from afar, then took our place on the rush-covered ground beside the drummers and witnessed the greeting of the sun.

What is grand in the character and appearance of the Indians is above all explained by the fact that for millennia they lived in a similarly grand and well-nigh measureless world of Nature and a priori saw in it their sanctuary and their way to the Divine.

Something that I had forgotten to mention is that after the morning prayer of the sponsor—the man who convened the Sun Dance and made the preparations for it—glowing coals are placed in two pits in the ground, first in the southern part of the Lodge and then in the northern; then evergreen branches are laid on top of them, so that thick clouds of incense arise. One dancer after the other bends over the smoke, holds his hands and also his feet over it, and then rubs his face and body in order to purify himself. The whole Lodge is filled with a pine-like fragrance.

Yesterday the relatives of the dancers brought quantities of fresh, sap-filled herbs, as well as fresh rushes, and gave them to the dancers; from these they made themselves cool places to rest. Today, on the last day of the ceremony, the dancers no longer have the right to alleviations of this sort.

In the late afternoon the extraordinarily virile drumming resounds for the last time, as does also the powerful and at the same time magical and jubilant song, accompanied by the thin fluting of the eagle-bone whistles. Then, all at once, there is silence; the Sun Dance comes to an end. We stand at the entrance; water is brought to the participants, from which they may drink a little three times; then, above the

PLATE XV

heads of the crowd, we see an arm lifted up, praying, blessing, conjuring. Each individual dancer is thus released from his Sun Dance oath, is freed from the sacred vow of the Dance; we see how they are blessed and how they are prayed over with uplifted hands, how they are fanned, stroked and touched with eagle feathers and bundles of sage. Finally the dancers are given gifts, each receives a blanket; at last they come out, and we welcome the completely exhausted Yellowtail. The Bannock chief makes a speech, first in the language of his tribe, and then in English for the benefit of the Indians from other tribes; in the name of his people, he thanks the organizers, the dancers, the drummers, the singers and the guests.

We ask Yellowtail if he suffered greatly from the terrible heat; yes, he answered, but round about the sacred Tree the earth had been cool.

The dancers had been brought four buckets of water with a little white clay in it; the sponsor touched the trunk of the Tree with his eagle fan and then dipped it into each bucket.

CONTINUATION OF THE JOURNEY

The Indians are often reproached with having no clear picture of the Hereafter; the reason for this is the same as in the case of Shintoism: a sharply defined eschatology is in nowise necessary here, in that a good Hereafter is guaranteed by a good here-below; hence the inflexibility of the Indian and Shintoist teachings on virtue and duty.

If there were no longer any Indians, if all that was Indian were to disappear, yet would the Indian spirit survive in God's immeasurable, wild and virginal Nature; it would live on in this vast, blissful prairie, in storm and soft wind, in rock and lightning flash, in all the rivers, streams, woods and mountains; in the radiant day and the silent night.

In Lodge Grass,[9] a secret society of the Crow—known as the Tobacco Society—was holding a festival. Everything was authentically Indian, as at the Sun Dance at Fort Hall: rapid, rhythmic drumming; powerful songs, warlike and at the same time magical; women in gay-colored blankets with green branches in their hands—the frontmost one had a wreath of leaves on her head and held a Sacred Pipe—rites, the performance of which is determined by the sacred number four, then distribution of gifts, and finally the evening meal of the initiates in a large tipi, open below and decorated with foliage.

In the early morning, as the sun rose, we heard a wonderful singing. My wife went out and in a short while returned: the old man who sang so marvelously in the Indian way in greeting to the sunrise, awakens his people each morning thus, telling them to arise, pray and remember their dead.

The last time I was in a tipi camp—at the festival of the Tobacco Society at Lodge Grass—the wonderful symbolism of the Indian tent became quite clear to me: two halves, two worlds, two realities, one below and one above—as in the hourglass—and between them an opening, a "strait gate"; in the tipi, the tent poles cross at this very point, separating outwards from one another into space and thus sym-

---

9. Montana, on the Crow Reservation.

bolizing Infinity. Below, Earth; above, Heaven; in the middle, a Gordian knot, a spiritual labyrinth; the crossing point of the tent poles, carefully arranged according to definite rules, is the soul's path to Heaven.

When, after the last Sun Dance prayer, Yellowtail explained the use of the Sacred Pipe, he first of all moved the pipe stem from side to side, holding it pointed towards Earth, in order to offer the Pipe to all Earth's creatures and so enable all to share in it; then he turned the pipe stem upwards, moved it from side to side, and said that this was for Heaven—for the stars and for the birds.

This distinction between stars and birds is significant: in the first case it is a reference to the higher and static possibilities and in the second, to the lower and dynamic possibilities in the heavenly world; the former are the immutable celestial archetypes and the latter are the "rays" therefrom which act directly on creatures, for example, heavenly messengers and guardian angels.

For the Indians, the angels act mainly through animals. The divine Proto-animal speaks through his earthly likeness.

Indian singing proceeds from principles different from those of European singing; the latter proceeds from man as such—or in a more profound sense, from the Divine within man—whereas the former above all humanizes the sounds of Nature, somewhat as Far Eastern music does, and thereby includes all creatures in the human voice; whence the roaring, croaking, cooing and speaking, the combination of thunder, storm, rushing water, neighing of horses and warbling of birds. The way to the Great Spirit goes back through the pre-human creations.

And thus, because Indian singing corresponds to a spiritual reality, it possesses the magic and beauty of the sounds of Nature; it is a human exultation which contains within it all the austerity of Nature; it belongs to the North American wilderness in the same way as the cry of gulls belongs to the sea, or the howling of the wind belongs to rocky mountains, or the cry of the eagle belongs to lonely, craggy heights.

Journey to America–1963

SECOND VISIT TO THE LAKOTA

In the evening we attended a dance festival at Wounded Knee;[10] as at the Sun Dance, there was a large circular ground with a pole in the center and shades all the way round; nearby, three tipis, a painted shield and a feathered lance had been set up; a painted buffalo skull was also there.

Fools Crow[11] was also there, in splendid dress adorned with long fringes and a war bonnet flowing to the ground—an apparition which combined eagle and sun, and at the same time had something of the powerful heaviness of the buffalo. He danced like a mountain in motion; coupled with this there was his grandiose, stone-like face. Seldom have I seen anything so unequivocal and powerful. The big drum thundered; the singing resounded, monotonous and yet with bold upward and downward movements; and all the while, there was lightning everywhere along the horizon. One was transported into a timeless past, when Heaven still touched Earth. And then that crowd of

---

10. South Dakota, on the Pine Ridge Reservation.

11. The famous Sioux medicine man. See the book *Fools Crow* by Thomas E. Mails (Doubleday & Co., New York, 1979).

PLATE XVI

swarthy people, often with faces of ravishing beauty; the impression is as fresh and amazing as it was on the first day.

All these handsome people, whose faces often seem to combine Far Eastern and Ancient Egyptian mystery, and at the same time evoke Mayan masks. I am reminded of the words of Queen Victoria when she saw Indians for the first time: "I have traveled widely and have seen many countries and peoples, but I have never seen better-looking people than these."

Early in the morning, a visit from Red Cloud, who wanted to say good-bye to us. He spoke moving words about the changes in the times: how in the old days a man wished to die in battle, and how he had now to grow old without deeds; how one no longer knew how to teach the children, and how they were corrupted in the schools. Only the Great Spirit could help in all this. When the time is ripe, we added.

CROWS, BLACKFEET AND CHEYENNES

We stopped at the famous rock formation which the Sioux call "The Home of the Bear" (Mato Tipila), and for which the palefaces could find no better name than "Devils Tower." This gigantic rock, as if it had grown out of the earth, reminds one of a Hindu temple and in a certain manner also of a Gothic cathedral; the red man venerates it as a holy place and explains the deep, regular, vertical grooves by the clawing of a monstrous bear. Black Elk counseled us to meditate at this place. Perhaps this miraculous rock was for the earlier Indians the center of the world; it is at all events the center of North America. Here one might receive inspirations from the Great Spirit, Black Elk told us, and all wild animals were tamer and friendlier. In fact a species of small marmot (the prairie dog) lives here, and these animals are exceedingly tame.

We traveled the whole day through endless, undulating prairie land, with mountains in the distance. Towards evening we reached the reservation of the Blackfeet.[12] There we found a large encampment of painted tipis which with their long poles, some of them ornamented with ribbons, stood out against the glowing evening sky. A splendidly clad Indian—his costume was similar to the one worn by Fools Crow at Wounded Knee—performed a slow Omaha war dance to the thunder of the drums and a singing that leapt wildly like a flame.

A glorious morning in the Indian camp. The huge open space is almost empty; a few Indians ride around in beautiful old-time costumes and feather headdresses; it is an imposing sight—indeed one of the most beautiful there is. I stand near the Sun Dance Lodge and watch the scene: the painted tipis all around, the chiefs on horseback, sometimes a few festively attired women and, in the background, the Rocky Mountains.

Time and again, when we have been among members of the red race, we have had to admire the many extraordinary, and often ravishingly beautiful, faces. It is curious that this race has so many examples to offer of both perfect youthful beauty and perfect aged beauty.

---

12. In northwest Montana.

An Indian camp in the morning sun has something timeless, rejoicing and rejuvenating about it; one walks slowly across the large, sunny grounds, across the rough, yellow-green meadow, and breathes the pure, gently cooling wind; the Origin is near and the Center is near. And the nearness of God lies as it were in the pure, golden air.

The Indian world represents on this earth a value that is irreplaceable; it possesses something unique and enchanting. When one encounters it in its unspoilt forms, one is aware that it is something altogether different from chaotic savagery; that it is human greatness, and at the same time harbors within itself something mysterious and sacred, which it expresses with profound originality.

As I write—it is already midnight—I hear in the distance the powerful drumming of an Indian festival. A hundred years ago this drumming would have caused the blood of many a man to freeze in his veins.

Yesterday evening, at supper in the open air, a Crow couple whom we knew before, were present, along with their twelve-year-old daughter. We spoke of all sorts of things, including medicine men: one night two Crows were in a pit surrounded by many Sioux, who were waiting for morning so that they might kill the Crows. One Crow said to the other: "You are a medicine man; do something!" The medicine man replied: "After I have sung, stay behind me, keep firm hold of my clothes, and follow me with your eyes shut; on no account open your eyes!" And so it was done; the two flew away, and in the morning, when the Sioux were about to celebrate their victory, no trace of the Crows could be found. The Sioux said: "They must have had strong medicine!" That, Yellowtail added, was one of the true stories from the old days.

In the afternoon the Sun Dance Tree is fixed into the ground; then with much effort they mount the cross beams, which like the spokes of a wheel connect the Tree with the outer poles. Finally a huge eagle is attached to the east side of the Tree, and to the west side a buffalo skull stuffed with sacred sage and with tufts of hair still around the horns.

In the late evening the Sun Dance begins. The eagle-bone whistles pierce the darkness like Japanese flutes in a Shinto ceremony. Three times, moving in opposite directions, the dancers circle round the Sun Dance Lodge, which is now fully enclosed with green boughs, then they go in; a fire is lit, the drum booms, singing resounds, half solemn, half warlike; the whole of the wilderness is in it, the howling and the storm, pervaded with the sacred and the eternal. The brightly illuminated Tree stands out like gold in the darkness, high up the eagle hangs ghost-like as it silently turns, and on the other side hangs the buffalo skull; a few stars shine above. The dancers begin to move, some forwards and backwards, blowing their whistles; the effect is a combination of mysterious, almost unearthly sounds—half eagle cry in the lonely heights, half the sound of flutes in a sacred grove. The other participants stand motionless, vividly lit up by the flickering fire; some are as if turned to stone, and we feel compelled to look at them again and again, because they are so unlike anything that can be seen in our time; they are like a primordial age turned into stone.

Today before sunrise we were once again at the appointed place. As the drum began to sound, we entered the Sun Dance Lodge and

---

13. Held again at Fort Hall, Idaho, on the Shoshoni-Bannock Reservation.

PLATE XVII

seated ourselves on our blankets. Moving indeed is the greeting of the rising sun, with arms stretched out towards it; then follow a few plaintive songs around the slowly dying fire, and then a single prayer in Shoshoni. And at the same time the larks outside are singing, as if Heaven and Earth seek to unite in this one jubilation.

From the fire that has been kept burning throughout the night, glowing coals are taken and placed in two small pits where a kind of cedar is burnt as incense. The dancers come one after the other and bend with their blankets over the pits, so as to purify themselves in the incense. A wonderful fragrance fills the Sun Dance Lodge.

All the dancers were now painted; some had painted the whole of the upper part of their bodies yellow, others had yellow and red on their faces; the forehead usually yellow, with red around the eyes, and sometimes with spots or lightning streaks on face and limbs.

Such a day on the Sun Dance plain has a beauty and a depth of happiness difficult to describe. In the distance lie the hills, and yet further the higher mountains; the earth stretches far and wide with its grayish-yellow dust, its irregular grass and the many light gray-green tufts of sage; larks sing, sometimes an eagle circles high above; in a large semicircle around the sacred leaf-covered Lodge shades, tipis and other tents stand. The sun burns, yet there is sometimes a very light, refreshing breeze; and one is always enveloped in the omnipresent drumming and the half wild and howling, half monotonous sacred singing. Over all this lies a perfume of greatness, nearness of God and deep peace.

Yesterday in the early afternoon the Sun Dance ended. A considerable crowd of people had gathered at the entrance to the Lodge; a white horse stood ready for the Ute medicine man; the drumming and singing were more powerful than ever, trills and cries rent the air. Inside, all sorts of consecratory rites were taking place: water was offered to the Four Directions and sacrificed to the central Tree, behind a curtain the dancers slaked their thirst, then they were blessed by the medicine man, and the older ones among them blessed the younger ones with arms held high. I saw how Yellowtail blessed a younger fellow dancer; for a time he stood behind him with arms held high and eyes closed. There were more prayers in Shoshoni, and then a brief speech in English; at last the sun dancers came out, walking with dignity side by side.

After this, a concluding festival was taking place. The feather crowns waving in the night, along with the powerful drumming and the singing, yet plaintive in its monotony—all this transported us once again into a strange and yet familiar world; a world which we carry within us, because all that is spiritually real is ours from the first.

CONTINUATION OF THE JOURNEY

At the festival procession[14] in the morning, we saw an old Indian on horseback, riding by himself and singing in a loud, somewhat plaintive voice with a beseeching tone, while at the same time he waved an eagle wing in his hand. The whole of the plains lay in this song; endless expanse, glowing sunlight, howling storm at night. It was moving to see and to hear this embodiment of an age-old and yet timeless world, and also to comprehend this special destiny, this jubilation of endless space and this plaint of withering time.

---

14. At Crow Fair, held annually on the Crow Reservation.

In the early afternoon, the final stage of the Crow Fair began. The dancers were painted, which gave their faces a clay-like, lifeless look; ochre yellow, brick red and black predominated. The great drum was carried around behind them, and to its rhythm they walked along one after the other, their tomahawks, feathered coup sticks or eagle feathers swinging in time; behind them came the heads of a secret society and then the beautifully dressed women; singing resounded and cries were uttered. All the dancers wore on their heads the classic roach, made of abruptly rising porcupine or deer hair, adorned with two feathers, which recalls the ancient Greek helmet, with all manner of ornaments on their bodies and limbs. The impression made by these warriors as they marched to the rhythm of the drum was a powerful one; it possessed a kind of uncanny grandeur, and at the same time, when one beheld the long-winding procession with the richly attired women at the end, something solemn and indeed sacerdotal; also something fateful, transcending the individual.

Everyone who holds an important position must make gifts on the occasion of this festival. As this is an extremely costly affair, all the relatives contribute their share. The donor first of all goes once round the large circle with small, dancing steps. An old chief, with a feathered staff in his hand, walks behind him, singing a praise song, and after him follow the relatives who have helped him with the buying of the gifts. Next, the crier calls out the names of those who are to receive presents: firstly the oldest members of the tribe, venerable old men with white braids, then the singers. There are eight groups of about seven singers, who take turns during the festival, singing throughout the whole night; these groups come from the most diverse tribes. After the singers, other guests of honor from foreign tribes receive gifts, including ourselves, and then also widows and poor families. Each one receives a brightly striped woolen blanket and a quilt or a few yards of cloth. The old people, singing a song of thanks, go back to their places; the others shake hands with the donor. At the end of the "give-away" the drum sounds and all those who have received something dance round the circle. Then the honor of giving passes to someone else, and the whole ceremony starts over again from the beginning: women bring mountains of blankets and cloths into the center of the circle, names are called out, and praise songs are sung, until the heap of presents has disappeared and further new heaps are carried in.

As always, I have to admire the many beautiful faces round about me; whether old or young, man or woman, all have something fascinating about them. There too sits the very aged Plain Feather slowly smoking the Sacred Pipe with two feather-adorned old men.

DEPARTURE FROM THE LAKOTA

In the evening there is a festival in Rosebud.[15] The Iron Shell family receives us; first the son comes, then the father and finally the mother. Later we are introduced to the chief Hollow Horn Bear, a most dignified personage; he wears a magnificent costume, with long fringes and a war bonnet that sweeps down to the ground; in his hand he holds a fan of eagle feathers. During the dances, he walks around the area with slow, dance-like steps, and in so doing he has something of an apparition about him, if only from the tremendously impressive force of his costume; the massiveness of the mountains is here combined with the radiance of the sky, earthly greatness accompanies sun-like majesty.

The Indian is predisposed towards the suprasensible and strives to penetrate the hard wall of the sensible world, seeks openings where he can, and finds them chiefly in phenomena themselves, which indeed, in their contents, are nothing other than signposts to the suprasensible. Things are hard-frozen melodies from the Beyond.

---

15. South Dakota, on the Rosebud Reservation.

PART THREE

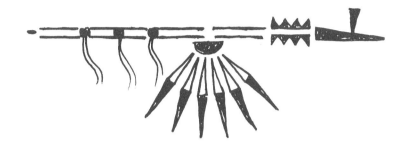

Excerpts From Correspondence

Excerpts from Correspondence

 The Indian religion of the Six Directions of space, and of Virgin Nature as Origin, and of Man as Center, is founded upon the six Primordial Truths, then upon the ontological holiness of Creation and upon the spiritual holiness of Man. Man is the great return: we must contain all of Creation and bring it back to the Divine Origin. He is the Altar and the Athanor: whence the Calumet and the Sun Dance. The cosmogonic flux stops at man and returns—in the inward Dimension—to the All-Powerful Creator, to the Unique Being, to the Indivisible Self.

To the North correspond winter, cold, night, old age; all this is Death or Purity.

To the South correspond summer, heat, day, maturity; all this is Life or Goodness.

To the East correspond spring, mildness, morning, youth; all this is Awakening, Victory, Liberation.

To the West correspond autumn, coolness, evening, aging; all this is Calm, Contemplativeness, Recollectedness, inward Beauty.

To the East also belong the dryness of the Act and the invincible Light; to the West, Humidity and Rain the bearer of graces, the gift of tears, the appeasing twilight.

The Sun is the Truth coming from God, manifesting God, and illuminating; the Moon is the Truth that warns, that reminds. Fire is devouring Knowledge; Water is conserving Love or Faithfulness, conserving Consciousness.

Lightning is Revelation; Rain is Grace; Wind is the Spirit.

The Red Indian culture is grounded on the unwritten, altogether non-theological wisdom of God's free Nature, its Book is the totality of God-created beings and things, beginning with the sacred Directions.

The Indian world signifies first and foremost the reading of the primordial doctrine in the phenomena of Nature—each man reads what he can understand—and the experiencing of Nature as the holy, primordial Home that everywhere manifests the Great Spirit and everywhere is filled with Him; and this consciousness gives the Red Man his dignity, composed of reverence for Nature and of self-dominion; it also throws light on the singular majesty of his artistically richly-accented appearance, in which eagle and sun combine and which, in the archetypal realm, belongs to the divine prototypes.

When we were adopted into the Lakota tribe, we received a small shield with the head of a stag, front view, painted on it; this was the credential of our membership in the tribe. Now, the stag is a priestly animal; it is the incarnation of the forest, which is in itself a sanctuary; its antlers are like a prayer, and when it leaps swiftly along it seems to float above the earth. With reference to one of the Psalms, the deer has been regarded as a symbol of the soul thirsting after God; and in many stories of saints it is the bearer of a message from Heaven.

The reason that so many Indians—including the famous medicine man Fools Crow, whom I met at Wounded Knee—practice both religions at once [Christianity and their own], or rather add Christianity to their own, is that the person of Christ appears to them as an irresistable spiritual reality, and they see no reason not to integrate Him into their religious life; they see no contradiction in this. I am speaking here of Indians who practice both religions, not of those who are wholly converted to Christianity, nor of those who refuse it totally.

In the spiritually far-off world of the American Indians—which is basically a prolongation of Mongolian Shamanism—a characteristic personification of the *Shakti* is the "White Buffalo Cow Woman" who brought the Calumet to the tribe of the Lakota Indians.[1] In her celestial substance, she is the goddess Wohpe, who is the equivalent of the Hindu goddess Lakshmi; in her earthly apparition she is called Pte-San-Win, the "White Buffalo Cow Woman," precisely. A few centuries ago, perhaps—no one knows the time or place—she appeared on earth

---

1. One no doubt meets with analogous if not the same accounts in other Indian tribes. In any case, the general symbolism has precedence over the particular "myth."

dressed in white or red, or completely naked, according to another tradition; the color white, like nudity, refers to primordiality, and the color red refers to life, success, happiness. And it is always the goddess Wohpe who brings the smoke of the Calumet to Heaven, in that cloud containing man's offerings and prayers; offerings, because sacred tobacco is made of various ingredients symbolizing the elements of the universe, for the prayer of an individual must be implicitly that of the collectivity and even that of the entire world.

The rite of the Calumet evokes the symbolism of the sacrificial smoke, that which rises from altars: all ritual smoke is a support of the ascending grace offered by the merciful *Shakti*, as the Hindus would say; the same is true of the incense that carries our praises towards Heaven. For the American Indians, incense—the "sweet" grass of the prairie or some other aromatic plant—has a purifying function: every sacred object is purified before being used, including the human body prior to a rite such as the Sun Dance. Smoke is the sacramental material used by the celestial Mediatrix; incense is like a veil that both envelops and manifests the invisible body of the goddess.

Smoke is an image of the breath; if the ritual smoke is sacred, so a fortiori is our breath whenever it is the vehicle of the Remembrance of God. And there is also a relationship between smoke and perfume; in the case of incense—including that of the Indians—both symbolisms are combined. Perfume expresses what in Arabic is termed *barakah*, which is not other than celestial or spiritual perfume; it emanates not only from saints and sacred things, but also from all that is agreeable to God, such as good actions and virtuous attitudes.

A fundamental quality of the Indians is liberality combined with disdain for riches; the Indian is not only very hospitable, he also loves to give, and sometimes gives almost all that he possesses; this is even a

PLATE XVIII

point of honor for the chiefs; whence the "give-away" feasts, where presents are given with the greatest generosity.

Strength, that vanquishes, and detachment, that gives. In the soul: victory over oneself and gift of self.

Indian dress "humanizes" Virgin Nature, thus it transmits something of the immensity of the prairies and the depth of the forests. It would be a mistake, be it said in passing, to object that this dress has merely a limited social and practical import, that not everybody wears it, that most often the Indian is more or less naked; that this dress comprises very different versions according to region, and moreover, that it has undergone considerable modifications over time and often in accordance with outward circumstances, and so on. What counts here are not these contingencies, but solely the Indian genius which, if it may express itself in diverse ways, always remains faithful to itself in its authentic productions.

To wear a traditional and sacred garment to which one has a sufficient right, is to be invested with an archetype and virtuality of perfection. . . .

A priori, dress is the outward, hence exoterism; but it is interiorized and becomes esoteric through its symbolical elements, its sacerdotal language precisely. In a certain respect, dress represents the soul when the body is considered only in its aspect of outwardness.

Since I have spoken of dress and its moral and spiritual exigencies, I must add certain reflections on nudity—by definition sacred—considered from the same standpoint. For here too, "noblesse oblige": the human body—like man as such—being "made in the image of God," manifests the universal qualities and therefore all of the virtues; it is essentially vertical and total, which amounts to saying that it is essentially noble. What is most outward expresses what is most inward—that is why Lalla Yogishwari,* having realized the Center, danced naked—so that the body reminds man of the celestial Norm and of the early Law. "Extremes meet. . . ."

The Indians . . . almost daily court suffering and death, and cultivate courage, self-control and dignity, while feeling they are everywhere before the Great Spirit; . . . they have by that very fact a certain grandeur which, combined with the extreme expressivity of their vestimentary and other art, explains the fascination that they inspire, and that sort of cult of which they are the object in the most diverse countries, and not merely among children, needless to say. . . .

The entire dress of the chief or the hero suggests the eagle soaring towards the sun: the shirt is the eagle, the sleeves with the fringes representing the wings; the feathered headdress is the sun. The nature of the eagle is to fly upwards, hence also to see things from afar, "from above" precisely; the eagle ascends and soars. The Sun Dance realizes the ascension of the royal bird towards the solar luminary . . . . When the Indian prays, he extends his arms upwards, like a bird taking wing. And I repeat here that to put on a costume is to be clothed with an archetype, a spirit.

According to an almost universal tradition, the eagle itself symbolizes the sun; this is expressed by the headdress of eagle feathers. Each feather must be won; the identification of man with the sun comprises

---

* Translator's note: a woman Kashmiri saint of the 14th century.

a heroic aspect, it implies a multiple victory over inferior *māyā.* as the Hindus would say, that of the world and that of the soul, spiritually speaking. . . .

All too often one imagines that the decorative style of the Red Indians only consists of geometric designs, but that is not at all the case, for this style is on the contrary, very precise and original, whatever the techniques by which it is manifested, and independently of the variety of its modes. It is in fact an essentially feminine art, as regards the artists; the art of the men is above all figurative—with the exception of the feathered sun—and serves to adorn tipis and robes, and sometimes shields and clothing. I will add that in all traditional art there are two poles: the symbolic content due to the immanent intellect, and the stylization due to the racial soul.

Sometimes one says that the Indians do not want to remain Indians and that they are partly responsible for their situation; this is hypocritical and murderous nonsense, for every people in the universe, treated as the Indians have been and living in the same conditions, would act in the same contradictory manner; it is not the Indians' fault that their traditional authorities have been practically abolished. We cannot put a ball on a slope as if it could stay there, and then, seeing that it falls down, pretend that it does so by its own will, without having been obliged to do so.

And thus, because Indian singing corresponds to a spiritual reality, it possesses the magic and beauty of the sounds of Nature; it is a human exultation which contains within it all the austerity of Nature; it belongs to the North American wilderness in the same way as the cry of gulls belongs to the sea, or the howling of the wind belongs to rocky mountains, or the cry of the eagle belongs to lonely, craggy heights.

The young Indians must not forget that they have a sacred patrimony to safeguard, and that nothing is more false than to admire the modern world and to scorn the sacred heritage of their race. If the former Indians had faults and made mistakes, it should be said that the same thing is true for all men, and that the imperfections of the Indians in former times were not worse than certain vices of the men of today, to say the least.

It is difficult to bear the sight of all the injustices of this world. But this earthly world will disappear anyway, and the most important thing is always spiritual life; if we cannot change the world around us, we can at least change ourselves. The essential teaching of every true religion is that this world of vanishing phenomena is unreal like a dream and that the unseen world of the Great Spirit is real. There are many degrees in the Unseen, but I just want to point out that there is more reality in the Unseen above than on this visible earth, and that God alone is absolute Reality.

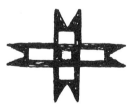

Index

BY THE SAME AUTHOR

THE TRANSCENDENT UNITY OF RELIGIONS, *FABER AND FABER, 1953*
REVISED EDITION, HARPER & ROW, 1974
THE THEOSOPHICAL PUBLISHING HOUSE, 1984

SPIRITUAL PERSPECTIVES AND HUMAN FACTS, *FABER AND FABER, 1954*
PERENNIAL BOOKS, 1969
NEW TRANSLATION, *PERENNIAL BOOKS, 1987*

LANGUAGE OF THE SELF, *GANESH, 1959*

GNOSIS: DIVINE WISDOM, *JOHN MURRAY, 1959*

STATIONS OF WISDOM, *JOHN MURRAY, 1961*
PERENNIAL BOOKS, 1980

UNDERSTANDING ISLAM, *ALLEN AND UNWIN, 1963, 1965, 1976, 1979, 1981*
PENGUIN BOOKS, 1972

LIGHT ON THE ANCIENT WORLDS, *PERENNIAL BOOKS, 1966*
WORLD WISDOM BOOKS, 1984

IN THE TRACKS OF BUDDHISM, *ALLEN AND UNWIN, 1968*

DIMENSIONS OF ISLAM, *ALLEN AND UNWIN, 1969*

LOGIC AND TRANSCENDENCE, *HARPER & ROW, 1975*
PERENNIAL BOOKS, 1984

ISLAM AND THE PERENNIAL PHILOSOPHY, *WORLD OF ISLAM*
FESTIVAL PUBLISHING COMPANY, 1976

ESOTERISM AS PRINCIPLE AND AS WAY, *PERENNIAL BOOKS, 1981*

CASTES AND RACES, *PERENNIAL BOOKS, 1981*

SUFISM: VEIL AND QUINTESSENCE, *WORLD WISDOM BOOKS, 1981*

FROM THE DIVINE TO THE HUMAN, *WORLD WISDOM BOOKS, 1982*

CHRISTIANITY/ISLAM: ESSAYS ON ESOTERIC ECUMENICISM,
WORLD WISDOM BOOKS, 1985

THE ESSENTIAL WRITINGS OF FRITHJOF SCHUON (S. H. NASR, ED.)
AMITY HOUSE, 1986

SURVEY OF METAPHYSICS AND ESOTERISM, *WORLD WISDOM BOOKS, 1986*

IN THE FACE OF THE ABSOLUTE, *WORLD WISDOM BOOKS, 1989*